A Ghastly-Good
HALLOWEEN

Gooseberry Patch Co.®

This book is dedicated to:

_____

Oxmoor House®

BRAVE INK PRESS

EDITORIAL STAFF

President and Editorial Director:
Carol Field Dahlstrom
Art Director: Lyne Neymeyer
Contributing Writer: Carol McGarvey
Photo Stylists: Carol Field Dahlstrom, Jennifer
Peterson, Jan Temeyer
Craft Designers: Susan Banker, Heidi Boyd,
Susan Cage, Katie LePorte, Janet Petersma,
Jan Temeyer, Megan Thompson
Director, Test Kitchen: Jennifer Peterson
Test Kitchen Professionals: Holly Wiederin,
Barbara Hoover
Copy Editor: Jill Philby
Proofreader: Elizabeth Burnley
Photography: Jay Wilde Photography;
Primary Image, Dean Tanner
Video/Communications: Dr. Michael Dahlstrom

BUSINESS STAFF

Business Manager: Judy Bailey
Webmaster: Leigha Bitz
Production Manager: Dave Hollingsworth
Props Manager: Roger H. Dahlstrom
Marketing: Marcia Schultz Dahlstrom

www.braveink.com

ISBN-13: 978-0-8487-3714-6
ISBN-10: 0-8487-3714-8
10 9 8 7 6 5 4 3 2 1

OXMOOR HOUSE

VP, Publishing Director: Jim Childs
Editorial Director: Leah McLaughlin
Creative Director: Felicity Keane
Brand Manager: Vanessa Tiongson
Senior Editor: Rebecca Brennan
Managing Editor: Rebecca Benton

A Ghastly-Good Halloween

Editor: Ashley T. Strickland
Project Editor: Laura Hoxworth
Director, Test Kitchen: Elizabeth Tyler Austin
Assistant Directors, Test Kitchen: Julie Christopher,
Julie Gunter
Test Kitchen Professionals: Wendy Ball, R.D.;
Victoria E. Cox; Margaret Monroe Dickey; Stefanie
Maloney; Callie Nash; Catherine Crowell Steele;
Leah Van Deren
Recipe Editor: Alyson Moreland Haynes
Photography Director: Jim Bathie
Senior Photo Stylist: Kay E. Clarke
Photo Stylist: Katherine Eckert Coyne
Assistant Photo Stylist: Mary Louise Menendez
Assistant Production Manager: Diane Rose
Contributing Test Kitchen Professionals: Tamara Goldis,
Erica Hopper, Callie Nash, Kathleen Royal Phillips
Contributing Interns: Erin Bishop; Maribeth Browning;
Mackenzie Cogle; Jessica Cox, R.D.; Alicia Lavender;
Anna Pollock; Ashley White

TIME HOME ENTERTAINMENT INC.

Publisher: Richard Fraiman
VP, Strategy & Business Development: Steven Sandonato
Executive Director, Marketing Services: Carol Pittard
Executive Director, Retail & Special Sales: Tom Mifsud
Director, Bookazine Development & Marketing:
Laura Adam
Publishing Director: Joy Butts
Finance Director: Glenn Buonocore
Associate General Counsel: Helen Wan

Our Story

Back in 1984, we were next-door neighbors raising our families in the little town of Delaware, Ohio. Two moms with small children, we were looking for a way to do what we loved and stay home with the kids too. We had always shared a love of home cooking and making memories with family & friends and so, after many a conversation over the backyard fence, Gooseberry Patch was born.

We put together our first catalog at our kitchen tables, enlisting the help of our loved ones wherever we could. From that very first mailing, we found an immediate connection with many of our customers and it wasn't long before we began receiving letters, photos and recipes from these new friends. In 1992, we put together our very first cookbook, compiled from hundreds of these recipes and, the rest, as they say, is history.

Hard to believe it's been over 25 years since those kitchen-table days! From that original little Gooseberry Patch family, we've grown to include an amazing group of creative folks who love cooking, decorating and creating as much as we do. Today, we're best known for our homestyle, family-friendly cookbooks, now recognized as national bestsellers.

One thing's for sure, we couldn't have done it without our friends all across the country. Each year, we're honored to turn thousands of your recipes into our collectible cookbooks. Our hope is that each book captures the stories and heart of all of you who have shared with us. Whether you've been with us since the beginning or are just discovering us, welcome to the Gooseberry Patch family!

Your friends at Gooseberry Patch

We couldn't make our best-selling cookbooks without YOU!

Each of our books is filled with recipes from cooks just like you, gathered from kitchens all across the country.

Share your tried & true recipes with us on our website and you could be selected for an upcoming cookbook. If your recipe is included, you'll receive a FREE copy of the cookbook when it's published!

www.gooseberrypatch.com

We'd love to add YOU to our Circle of Friends!

Get free recipes, crafts, giveaways and so much more when you join our email club...join us online at all the spots below for even more goodies!

Email Club · Blog · You Tube · f · t · p · Find a Store

contents

36

75

"When witches go riding, and black cats are seen, the moon laughs and whispers, 'tis near Halloween."

— ANON

Chapter 1

A Patchwork of Pumpkins

(Boo-oodles of Thrilling Ideas!)

Pumpkins take center stage when it's time for Halloween! Whether they are carved, painted, embellished or just piled in the back of the truck, they signal that Halloween is near! These spirited squash can be carved to be frightful or painted to be a piece of pumpkin art. Add some rhinestones and scraps of fabric, and your little gourd may become gorgeous.

With just a pinch of imagination and some crafting magic, your pick-of-the-patch pumpkin will transform into a glowing Jack-O'-Lantern...a masterpiece of fun and fright to share this Halloween!

*"I would rather sit on a **pumpkin**, and have it all to **myself**, than be crowded on a **velvet cushion**."*

— HENRY DAVID THOREAU

Creepy (and clever) Carved & Cutout Pumpkins

CARVING PUMPKINS is a Halloween ritual that everyone enjoys. Whether you like to cut off the top and pull out the seeds, or you prefer to carefully etch in the pumpkin design with a tiny blade, pumpkin carving is a Halloween art. So gather up your carving tools and let the fun begin! For more tips on carving pumpkins, see page 22.

BOO PUMPKINS

Choose your favorite frightening font to carve into a bright orange pumpkin. Or spell a Halloween greeting to welcome your guests. Glue some white pearl buttons beside the carved letters for some vintage style.

HAUNTED HOUSE PUMPKIN

They'll be shivering in their boots when they are greeted at the door by this spooky haunted house! Choose a large pumpkin for this design to give enough room for the fine detail. Cut off the top and scoop out the insides of the pumpkin. Then draw the house you like on the pumpkin with pencil first. Or copy the pattern we have used onto the pumpkin. (See page 186 for the pumpkin pattern.) Then carve away! The little windows and door are only carved through the first layer of the pumpkin skin allowing for less light to show through and creating an eerie sight!

"As Spirits roam the neighborhoods at night,
Let loose upon the Earth till it be light."

— NICHOLAS GORDON

MR. MARBLE EYES PUMPKINS
These little buddies are so easy to make, and each has its own special personality! Marbles of different sizes, shapes and colors serve as eyes, and smiles can be as sinister, silly or serious as you like! Choose a gray pumpkin with orange flesh if you want your pumpkin's smile to really shine! For pumpkin face ideas, see pages 186–187.

JACK-'O-PIGGY AND JACK-'O-PRETTY GIRL PUMPKINS

This duo of pumpkins are carved with simple faces and add-on pieces. Cut off the top and scoop out the insides. Use a pumpkin tool to carve the faces. Then add on some little 3-D features. *For the piggy,* cut a slice from the underside of the lid to make the snout. Punch two holes in the snout. Secure in place with a ½" piece of toothpick. *For the pretty girl, f*or the eyes and earrings, cut circles using a fruit coring tool from the cutout pumpkin scraps, trimming off the back. Use ½" pieces of toothpicks to hold the eyes and earrings in place. For teeth, cut slits in the mouth area and insert pumpkin seeds to resemble teeth. For pumpkin face ideas, see pages 186–187.

CATS, RATS & BATS!

This eerie pumpkin is carved into the first layer of the pumpkin after the pumpkin has been painted black. Simply trace around the pattern onto the dry painted pumpkin. Then use a wood carving tool to cut away the negative space, leaving the cat, bats and rat! For the pattern for this pumpkin, see page 189.

TOGETHERNESS PUMPKINS

Three little pumpkins team up to make a happy trio of smiling pumpkins. Choose 3 pumpkins about the same size. Cut off the tops and scoop out the insides of each pumpkin. Draw the faces on the pumpkins first with pencil. Then carefully cut out the expressions with a pumpkin carving tool. Set the pumpkins side by side in the order you like and make a mark where they touch. Cut a slice from both sides of the middle pumpkin and one side of each of the other pumpkins. Set the pumpkins back together. For pumpkin face ideas, see pages 186–187.

*"Produce great **pumpkins**, the **pies** will follow later."*

— ANON

Petrifyingly Painted
(yet preposterous) Pumpkins

IF YOU WANT YOUR PUMPKIN creations to last for the season…grab the paints and brushes! Painted pumpkins are perfect for decorating indoors and out, and each one can have its own pumpkin personality! You can use flat paint, spray paint, dimensional paint and even metallic paint to get the look you want. Look to candies, printed fabric or nature for design inspiration, and don't forget that fairy tales might inspire you to create that magical pumpkin!

BIRDIE TRIO PUMPKINS
Turn things around a bit for your Halloween pumpkin this year! Instead of setting the pumpkin on its bottom, turn it on its side and you'll see all kinds of possibilities! Use acrylic paint to paint the pumpkins first. Then add felt feathers, a little pumpkin hat and buttons for eyes.

CANDY CORN PUMPKINS

Here's a sweet idea! Get out the spray paint and make your own candy pumpkins! Choose pumpkins that are tall and thin. Then use masking tape to mask off the areas and spray paint each section, letting each color dry before moving to the next. You'll have a sweet candy pumpkin in no time!

BANDANNA-INSPIRED PUMPKINS

Let the designs on a bandanna inspire you to paint your pumpkins this fall. Start by painting the pumpkin gray. Paint paisley designs and dots on the pumpkin using dimensional paint in a tube. Add jewels for some extra sparkle, if you'd like.

Petrifyingly Painted (yet preposterous) Pumpkins

TIPS ON PAINTING PUMPKINS

With the array of paints available today, you will have all kinds of choices for painting your pumpkins. Choose an acrylic paint if you are using a brush. Acrylic paints come in hundreds of colors as well as metallic and pearl varieties. If you are using spray paint, choose a paint that is suitable for indoor or outdoor use. After the paint dries, your pumpkin will keep for several weeks.

*"The King's son, who was told that a **great princess**, whom nobody knew, was come, ran out to receive her. He gave her his **hand** as **she alighted** from the coach, and led her into the hall where the company were assembled."*

— CHARLES PERRAULT, 1628–1703

CINDERELLA'S COACH PUMPKIN

What could be more exciting than turning a humble squash into a glorious Cinderella carriage? Start by painting the pumpkin with white primer. Then work your magic by painting it with white pearl paint. Let dry. Paint a carriage door on the front with gold metallic paint. Let dry and then adhere bits of fabric trims and pearls to the door. Paint the stem gold, blending into the white pearl paint on the pumpkin.

Wrap fine gold wire around the pumpkin stem for texture. Add press-on jewels to the pumpkin and pearls around the stem for added princess-like sparkle. For the wheels, coil silver and white chenille stems. Add one more chenille stem between each set. Lay the wheels beside the pumpkin. As elegant as this carriage looks, you can create it in an evening…long before the clock strikes midnight.

JACK FROST PUMPKIN

Just as Jack Frost often surprises us with the first frost of winter, this pumpkin surprises us with its transformation from plain pumpkin to glorious gourd. To get the cool look, paint the pumpkin cobalt blue as the base coat. Then add a light coat of iridescent pearl paint. Use white paint to paint random snowflakes, and then paint another light coat of pearl paint over the top to look like frost. Add rhinestones to the snowflakes for snow-like shimmer.

Zebra-Striped
Pumpkin

Houndstooth
Pumpkin

Argyle Pumpkin

FASHION PUMPKINS

Whether you prefer zebra stripes, argyle or houndstooth, you'll love painting these pattern-inspired pumpkins. All of the pumpkins start with a white base coat. *For the Zebra-Striped Pumpkin,* paint black organic stripes on the pumpkin and paint the stem purple. *For the Houndstooth Pumpkin,* trace the pattern on page 194 onto the pumpkin. Paint every other shape black or white. Paint the background black and the stem light green. *For the Argyle Pumpkin,* trace the pattern, page 194 onto the pumpkin. Fill in the shapes with alternating paint colors. Let dry. Layer black dashed lines over the top of the painted design using a fine-point paint brush. Paint the stem black.

"Double, double, toil and trouble;
Fire burn and cauldron bubble."

— MACBETH BY WILLIAM SHAKESPEARE

Spectacularly Spooky (but sensational) Pumpkins

LOOK AROUND THE HOUSE for some fun embellishments to decorate your chosen pumpkin. Felt scraps, buttons, tacks, old hats and gloves are a few of the finds that might just turn that ho-hum pumpkin into a pumpkin with personality-plus!

COBWEB PUMPKIN

Paint-in-a-tube is the simplest way to accomplish this easy, yet creepy, cobweb design. Let the lines of the pumpkin guide you to paint the vertical lines of the cobweb. Then scallop the other lines across to create the simple design. Add a dusting of glitter and a friendly little sticker spider.

COOL COUPLE PUMPKINS

Invite a cool couple to your Halloween get-together! Carve out the pumpkins, add faces and then add upholstery tacks for a little sparkle in their eyes. Top him off with a baseball cap and her with a pair of gloves for a quick hair-do. For face pattern ideas, see pages 186–187.

Mrs. Pumpkin Head

MRS. PUMPKIN HEAD

Look in the felt scrap box for your inspiration to create a funny-faced pumpkin in no time! Felt shapes come in all sizes and motifs and can be purchased at discount and crafts stores. Let the kids help design a whole family of these silly pumpkin heads.

LACED-UP PUMPKIN

Let a drill do the carving for you, and then have fun lacing up this clever pumpkin. Cut off the top of the pumpkin and scoop out the insides and seeds. Use a pencil to mark where you want the holes. Then use a drill to make the holes in the pumpkin. Lace up the pumpkin using a wide cord or string.

RHINESTONE COWBOY PUMPKIN

A few self-stick rhinestones, a bandanna and cowboy hat are all you need to make this little pumpkin turn into a sparkling show stopper. Add a sheriff's badge if you like and you're ready to party, partner!

Rhinestone Cowboy Pumpkin

Laced-Up Pumpkin

A Pumpkin Patch of Information

PUMPKINS are downright versatile, and they just cry out, "It's autumn." You can eat them, decorate with them, carve them and simply smile at a pile of them. They come in all sizes and in colors from bright orange to red, white, blue-green and mixed colors.

Pumpkin varieties:

There are myriad kinds of pumpkins in the "cucurbita" family, which includes watermelon, many kinds of squash and cucumbers. Visit a pumpkin patch or orchard and be amazed by the huge variety. Names are fun, including Baby Boo, Casper and White Ghost for the white ones, and Baby Bear, Jack-Be-Little and Munchkin for miniature varieties.

Cucurbita Moschata – This grouping takes in crookneck squash, butternut squash and cushaw squash.

Cucurbita Pepo – This category includes the Jack-'O-lantern varieties, summer squashes, gourds, pattypan squash and zucchini.

Cucurbita Maxima – The "biggies" of the pumpkin patch fall into this group, along with Hubbard squash, Boston squash, banana squash and turban squash.

Cucurbita Mixta – "Fun" pumpkins, such as the little miniature varieties, white ones and the blue or blue-green varieties are in this category.

Pumpkin carving:

So much of the fun of Halloween involves carving your Jack-'O-lantern. You can cut it freehand, of course, or you can work with intricate stencils or patterns for special looks and effects. Stencils are available at crafts stores, in magazines and newspapers and from online sources.

Some carvers like to use special tools, but items you already have in your kitchen or workshop will work just fine. An ice cream scoop or larger spoon, a thin-blade knife and lots of newspaper will suffice.

To get started, cut out the top of the pumpkin around the stem or handle. Cut an opening big enough for your hand to fit inside the pumpkin so you can remove the membranes—some call them the "brains" of the pumpkin. As you cut the top, it works well to angle the knife, so that the stem or "hat" will fit back into the hole without falling into the pumpkin.

After the top is cut, pull it off and pull out as much membrane and seeds as you can. Use your scoop or large spoon to scrape out the rest.

Check out the pumpkin to see which side looks best for the front or face of the pumpkin. If you wish, use a pencil or marker to plan where the eyes, nose and mouth should be located. Carefully cut out the face parts. Or grab the drill for making holes or other designs in the pumpkin. Always be sure to clean your tools well when you are done, so that you are ready next year.

Be sure the inside bottom or base is level enough to hold a lighted candle inside of the Jack-'O-lantern. For safety, it works well to use a votive candle in a glass holder. White candles tend to offer the most light. Enjoy the look, but keep a close watch for safety's sake.

Did you know?

- The top pumpkin-producing states are Illinois, Ohio, Pennsylvania and California.

- Pumpkins are grown primarily for processing, with the rest going to ornamental sales at farmers' markets, you-pick farms and retail outlets.

- Pumpkins are used to make soups, pies, bars and breads.

- In early Colonial times, pumpkins were used to make crusts of pies, not the filling.

- Pumpkins were once thought to be able to remove freckles and cure snake bites.

- Pumpkins are considered a fruit.

- Pumpkins and their seeds are full of nutrients—Vitamins C, A and E; zinc, potassium, magnesium, iron, lutein (for healthy eyes) and alpha carotenoids (antioxidants that help prevent cell damage).

- Pumpkin seeds are a good source of protein.

- Pumpkin flowers are edible.

- Pumpkins range in size from one pound to more than 1,000 pounds.

- The name pumpkin came from "pepon," the Greek word for "large melon."

- Pumpkins are made up of 90 percent water.

- In the early 1800s, American pioneers and Native Americans used every part of the pumpkin. They roasted pumpkin strips over fires and used them for food. They roasted, baked, boiled and dried the pumpkin flesh. They ate pumpkin seeds and used them as medicine. They used the whole pumpkin, even adding the blossoms to stews and soups. After drying, pumpkin flesh was ground into flour for baking.

"We have pumpkins at morning And pumpkins at noon. If it were not for pumpkins, we should be undoon."

— PILGRIM VERSE, CIRCA 1633

TIPS ON CHOOSING PUMPKINS AND KEEPING PUMPKINS

A trip to the pumpkin farm or farmers' market is a must to pick just the right pumpkins for the season. Choose a pumpkin free of bruises or cuts that can often happen during harvest. These marks can let bacteria into your pumpkin and it will spoil sooner. Choose a stem that fits your decorating plan. Some pumpkin stems can be just as interesting as the pumpkin! Some are twisted, long, fat or curved.

To make your pumpkins last longer, wash them with hot soapy water when you get home from the farm or market. Then spray them with an all-purpose glass or surface cleaner to be sure all of the bacteria is killed. Store them in a cool, dry place, and your pumpkins should last the entire season.

Chapter 2

Bewitching Decorations

(Eeriesistible Ideas to Scare Them Silly!)

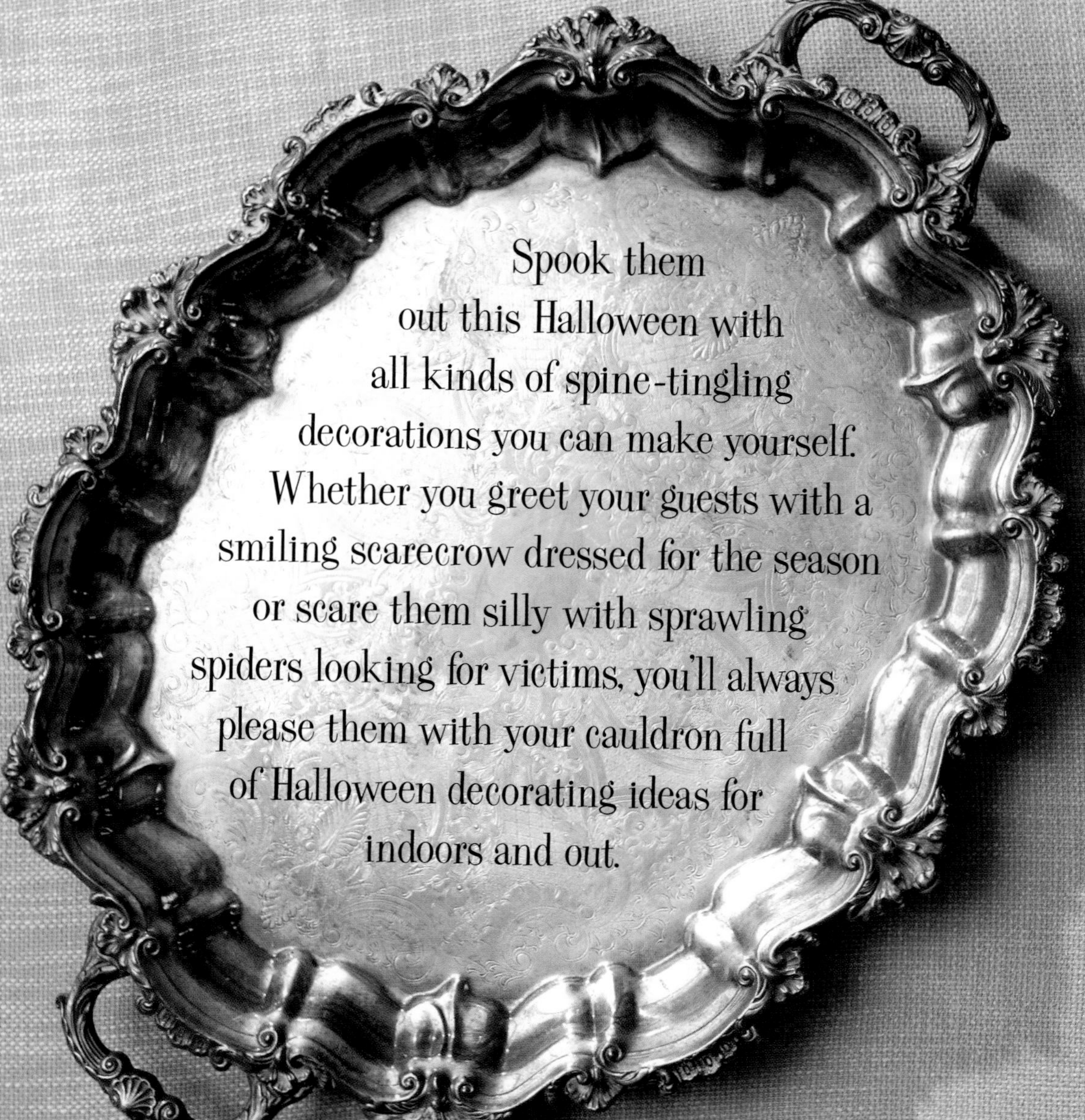

Spook them
out this Halloween with
all kinds of spine-tingling
decorations you can make yourself.
Whether you greet your guests with a
smiling scarecrow dressed for the season
or scare them silly with sprawling
spiders looking for victims, you'll always
please them with your cauldron full
of Halloween decorating ideas for
indoors and out.

*"There are **nights** when the **wolves** are silent and only the **moon howls.**"*

— GEORGE CARLIN

The Eyes Have It!

YOU MIGHT HEAR GHASTLY GIGGLES when they sit down to the Halloween table this year! Serve their treats on eyeball- or rib-inspired dishes. Then create a centerpiece with all kinds of unique body parts to examine. Reading the labels will keep them grinning all night long!

LIMBS & ORGANS CENTERPIECES

Fish bowls or other clear vessels become holders for the most interesting body parts! All these well-preserved parts are edible and quite delicious! Glue the fishbowl or vessel to a small glass dish or goblet to give it height, or use as is for the holder. Decoupage the labels to the outside of the glass. Then fill with all kinds of goodies! For labels to print, see page 190. For instructions, see page 173. For a closer look at the centerpieces and a list of what is *really* in them, turn the page.

FRESHLY STUBBED

INGROWN TOENAILS

Clipper Tested Since 1873

"Wool of bat, and tongue of dog, Adder's fork, and **blind-worm's sting.** *Lizard's leg, and howlet's wing. For a charm of powerful trouble, Like a hell-broth* **boil and bubble."**

– MACBETH BY WILLIAM SHAKESPEARE

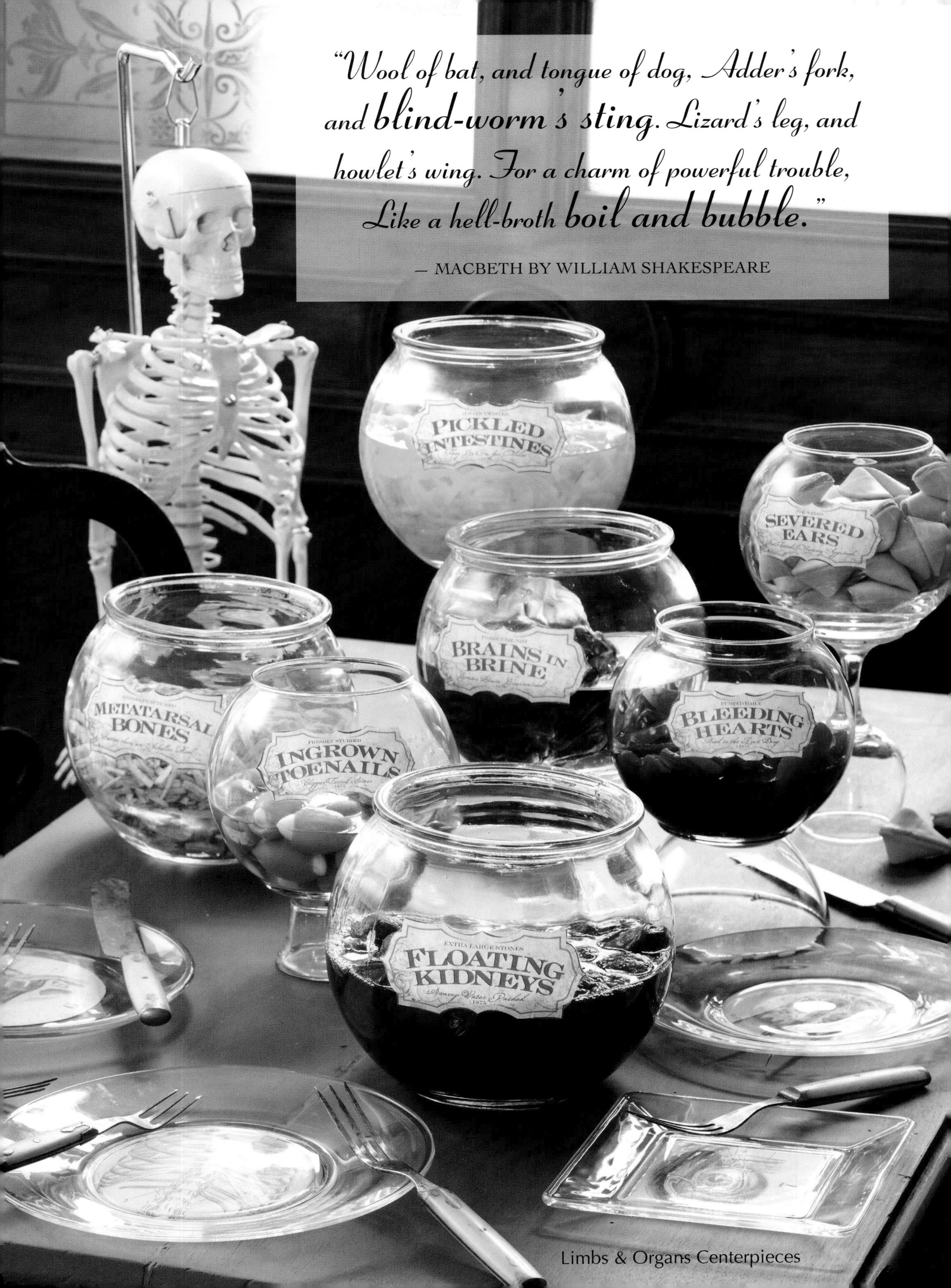
ALWAYS TWISTED
PICKLED INTESTINES
SEVERED EARS
FORGET-ME-NOT
BRAINS IN BRINE
METATARSAL BONES
FRESHLY STUBBED
INGROWN TOENAILS
PUMPED DAILY
BLEEDING HEARTS
EXTRA LARGE STONES
FLOATING KIDNEYS

Limbs & Organs Centerpieces

FORGET-ME-NOT
BRAINS IN BRINE
Genius Brain Guaranteed
1875

BLEEDING HEART

Limbs & Organs
Centerpieces

*"From **ghoulies** and ghosties And long-leggedy beasties, And things that go **bump** in the night, Good Lord, deliver us!"*

— SCOTTISH SAYING

BODY PARTS PLATES

Vintage images of medically correct body parts become the design on plates and dishes that share the Limbs & Organs goodies. The images are simply decoupaged on the backside of the dishes. Images to copy are on page 191. Instructions for making the dishes are on page 173.

Need some ideas for what to serve in your Limbs and Organs Centerpieces? Here is what is in our glass vessels:

BRAINS IN BRINE: small head of red cabbage in water

INGROWN TOENAILS: garlic stuffed olives

BLEEDING HEARTS: pickled beets cut into heart shapes

FLOATING KIDNEYS: canned red plums

PICKLED INTESTINES: pickled banana peppers

METATARSAL BONES: french fries in a can

SEVERED EARS: fortune cookies

Body Parts Plates

Skeleton Crew

GATHER UP THOSE BONES and have some bona fide fun making Halloween decorations! You'll have a captive audience when you arrange skulls for greetings and centerpieces. And there won't be any skeletons left in your closet when you make tables and place cards for your Halloween party!

SKULLDUGGERY CENTERPIECE

Purchased plastic skulls are painted and glittered to make a most memorable centerpiece. Set the colorful group on a tarnished silver tray around a black cauldron of dry ice to create a ghost-like mood.

CRANIUM TRIO

A vintage clothespin bag is snatched from the clothesline and used to hold a trio of Halloween skulls. Hang the filled-up bag on a door or window for an especially scary greeting.

Skullduggery Centerpiece

Cranium Trio

Rattle-Me-Bones
Place Cards

Them Bones Table

RATTLE-ME-BONES PLACE CARDS

Little bones set up just right when you glue them together to hold an initial letter for a place card at your Halloween table. The back of the card is a little tent that folds to hold the card. Instructions are on page 173.

THEM BONES TABLE

Let those femur bones become legs when they hold up a table top you've painted the same color. Little bones surround the top. Instructions are on page 173.

Pretty Posy Pumpkins

DECORATING WITH PUMPKINS is a must at Halloween. Add some floral fun this year by making pumpkins into lovely containers. Simply cut off the tops of the pumpkins and scoop out the inside. Fill with water and add a floral or herbal bouquet for all to enjoy!

POSY PUMPKIN CENTERPIECE

You can never have too many flowers! So why not carve a favorite posy on the outside of the pumpkin before you fill it with your favorite blooms? Carefully use a linoleum or wood cutting tool to carve a floral design just through the first layer of the pumpkin. The pumpkin will still hold water as the etched design decorates the pretty pumpkin.

Posy Pumpkin Centerpiece

HERBAL ARRANGEMENT

Pumpkins and gourds come in all sizes, shapes and colors. Choose a white pumpkin and scoop out the insides. Fill with water and add freshly cut herbs. Set the pumpkin on a plate and surround it with patterned gourds or squash. What a pretty and fresh arrangement!

PANSY PUMPKIN

Pansies are a cool-weather flower and work wonderfully for fall decorations. Cut scallops around the top of the scooped-out pumpkin. Then use an awl to make holes under each scallop. If you like, add a design under the hole using a linoleum cutter. Fill the pumpkin with water and float pansy blooms for a colorful centerpiece.

Pansy Pumpkin

Arachnophobia!

AN INVASION OF SPIDERS is just what you'll need to scare them silly this Halloween! Whether they are squirming in a birdcage, infesting your table or hanging from the ceiling, these little critters will set the mood. Make your own arachnid decorations with simple materials that won't leave you skittish about holding spiders.

BLACK BOA TARANTULAS

Chenille stems, beads and part of a feather boa combine to make eight-legged decorations for your table. Prop these everywhere you want to hear some screams! Instructions are on page 173.

BLOODCURDLING CANDLES & CANDLESTICKS

Candlesticks are adorned with painted black widow spiders crawling up the sides. Candles with blood-colored wax make the look complete! Instructions are on page 174.

"Tis the **night** *— the night Of the* **grave's** *delight, And the* **warlocks** *are at their play."*

— ARTHUR CLEVELAND COXE

Black Boa Tarantulas/
Bloodcurdling
Candles & Candlesticks

Scarecrows, Ghosts & Frightful Faces (oh my!)

FAVORITE YET FRIGHTENING Halloween motifs can set the stage for your Halloween decorating, indoors and out. Start by making a set of scarecrows to ward off the ravens. Then create your own vintage-style paper faces to decorate a wreath and a set of friendly ghosts to haunt your lawn.

SCARECROW COUPLE

Dress your scarecrow couple in a homespun frock and overalls or more sophisticated attire. Whatever you choose, you'll have fun setting this couple outside to scare away the crows and welcome your Halloween guests. Instructions for making the scarecrows are on page 176.

Scarecrow Couple

FRIGHTFUL FACES WREATH

Inspired by vintage Halloween decorations, the paper decorations on this wreath are made using shapes cut from colorful cardstock. Then they are simply tied to a purchased black wreath. For patterns to make the paper shapes, see pages 187–188.

GHOSTLY DUO

These little apparitions are quick to make using white fabric and liquid starch. Form them over a rose cone to get the original shape. Their not-too-scary expressions are simply cut from black felt and glued on with crafts glue. Instructions for making the ghosts are on page 176. Patterns for their faces are on page 189.

Frightful Faces Wreath

Ghostly Duo

Hallo-Wees

MAKE YOUR OWN team of little needle-felted friends to tuck into the crevices and corners of your house for some fun Halloween decorating. Each creepy little critter is made using wool roving and a felting needle. For complete instructions for all of the gang and how-to photos for needle-felting, see pages 174–176.

GIDEON GHOST & PETE PUNKIN

Ready to perch on any little pumpkin or shelf, this little duo is easy and fun to make. Gideon's tiny features are worked into the white roving using a felting needle. Little Pete Punkin is so tiny he can sit on the head of a pencil.

Gideon Ghost
& Pete Punkin

Lil' Count

Franklin-stein and
Franklin's Bride/
Mini Mummy

Witch Hazel

LIL' COUNT
Dressed for the occasion, this little Dracula has a red cape and white fangs…all made from wool.

FRANKLIN-STEIN AND FRANKLIN'S BRIDE
This delightfully scary pair is worked in many shades of wool. Frankie's Bride is slightly taller than Franklin…standing a tall 3 inches.

MINI MUMMY
White wool roving turns into bandages trimmed with just a tiny bit of charcoal wool to make this little guy.

WITCH HAZEL
A very detailed hat and a sweet smile makes this little gal as fun to create as she is to have around!

Chapter 3

Terrorific Part

What can be more fun than having a Halloween party to celebrate this scary and silly time of year? Whether you like to gather everyone at your home to play games, watch scary movies, have a cookie exchange, help the little ones have a blast or just enjoy the bounty of the season, you can plan the perfect party with some simple tricks and yummy treats you conjure up yourself. Everyone will be talking about the bootiful and bone-chilling party you shared this year!

(A Cauldron Full of Ideas They'll Love

Haunted Open House Party

Invite all the ghouls and gents in the neighborhood for a Halloween party that will frighten and delight! Set up a buffet and feature a Haunted Gingerbread Castle that will become the showpiece of the party. Then surround it with to-die-for goodies they'll love to devour!

Are you brave enough to venture out on All Hallows' Eve?

Come if you dare to our

Haunted Open House Party

Saturday, October 31st
8:00 PM until Midnight
13 Spooky Lane
Amherst

COME IF YOU DARE!

Getting Ready for the Party:
Your Haunted Gingerbread Castle can be made days before the party. Because it is made from gingerbread, it will keep for weeks. Plan how you want to set up your buffet table and how your guests can serve themselves.

Party Activities:
If your party includes people who may not often come to your home, make them feel comfortable by having a basket of disguises at the door. That way, if they didn't dress up in costume for the party, they can still join in the fun by choosing a simple costume to wear. For an easy game, play some music with some Halloween themes, and then have the guests "Name that Tune." The winner gets some extra candy!

The Invitation:
Create a Halloween invitation that will haunt them…and one that they can't resist! The round paper moon is inked on the edges and the haunted house is a simple cutout pattern. All of the information that the guests need to know comes sliding out on a little hidden brad. Make the envelope as inviting as the inside with a simple design stamped on a round circle. Instructions for making the Haunted House Invitation are on page 177 and the pattern in on page 192.

Tablescapes:
Set up the buffet using an orange tablecloth. Then use a combination of metal platters and crockery bowls to hold all the goodies. Add some cobwebs to the windows and doors behind the table to make your house seem eerily haunted.

"Witch and ghost make merry on this last of dear October's days."
— ANON

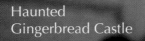

Haunted Gingerbread Castle

You can make this castle as elaborate, scary or silly as you like...but no matter how you make it, this castle will be a haunted, handmade beauty!

Gingerbread Dough

2 c. shortening
2 c. sugar
2 c. molasses
2 T. cinnamon
2 t. ground cloves
2 t. baking soda
1 t. salt
9 to 10 c. all-purpose flour

To make dough, heat shortening, sugar and molasses in a 5-quart saucepan over low heat until sugar dissolves, stirring constantly. Remove from heat; stir in cinnamon, cloves, baking soda and salt. Gradually work in flour until a stiff dough forms; turn dough out onto a lightly floured surface and knead in as much remaining flour as possible while still maintaining a smooth consistency. Divide into 4 sections; wrap each in plastic wrap and refrigerate until ready to use. Dough should chill for at least 2 hours before rolling out.

continued on page 56

Make a Haunted Gingerbread Castle to be the star of your open house party. The castle walls are made from baked gingerbread dough and held together with frosting. The turrets are ice cream cones and the spooky trees are candy coating poured into tree shapes and covered with sprinkles. Little wafer crackers form the shutters and frosted cookies add lots of "character" to this house. Make your haunted castle as simple as you like…or make it a wickedly-wonderful work of art. Complete instructions and how-to photos are on pages 56–57. The basic patterns for the house are on page 195.

Squishy Party Potatoes

These are the yummiest potatoes ever!

4 c. mashed potatoes
1 c. sour cream
8-oz. pkg. cream cheese, softened
1 t. dried chives
$\frac{1}{4}$ t. garlic powder
$\frac{1}{4}$ c. dry bread crumbs
1 T. butter, melted
$\frac{1}{2}$ c. shredded Cheddar cheese

In a large bowl, combine potatoes, sour cream, cream cheese, chives and garlic powder. Turn into a greased 2-quart casserole dish. Combine bread crumbs with butter; sprinkle over potatoes. Bake, uncovered, at 350 degrees for 50 to 60 minutes. Top with Cheddar cheese and serve. Serves 8 to 10.

Looking-at-You Meatballs

These tasty little morsels will be the hit of the party!

1 lb. ground pork sausage
$1\frac{1}{4}$ c. pork-flavored stuffing mix
$\frac{1}{2}$ c. low-sodium chicken broth
$\frac{1}{2}$ c. Honeycrisp apple, peeled, cored and diced
$\frac{1}{2}$ c. onion, diced
1 egg, beaten
$1\frac{1}{2}$ t. mustard
$\frac{1}{2}$ c. shredded sharp Cheddar cheese

In a large bowl, combine all ingredients. Form into balls by tablespoonfuls. Place on a lightly greased 15"x10" jelly-roll pan. Bake at 350 degrees for 18 to 20 minutes, until meatballs are no longer pink in the middle. Serves 8 to 10.

TRICK OR TREAT!

Here's a Trick:
Make the meatballs ahead of time and keep in a slow cooker until ready to serve.

Looking-at-You Meatballs

Cobweb Salad

Cobweb Salad

Let the spaghetti slide off the side of the bowl for a fun and web-like presentation.

16-oz. pkg. spaghetti, uncooked
2 cucumbers, peeled, seeded and diced
2 tomatoes, diced
3 green onions, chopped
½ green pepper, diced
½ red pepper, diced
8-oz. bottle sun-dried tomato vinaigrette salad
   dressing
salt and pepper to taste

Cook pasta according to package directions; drain and rinse with cold water. In a large bowl, combine pasta with remaining ingredients except salt and pepper. Toss well to coat. Refrigerate several hours or overnight before serving. Season with salt and pepper just before serving. Serves 6.

Orange Bone Slices

These carrots will be gobbled up…no matter how you slice them!

2 c. carrots, peeled and chopped
1 clove garlic, minced
1 t. dill weed
2 T. butter
salt and pepper to taste

Place carrots in a saucepan; add just enough water to cover. Bring to a boil over medium-high heat. Cook for 3 to 5 minutes, until tender; drain. Add remaining ingredients; reduce heat to medium. Sauté lightly until butter is melted and carrots are heated through. Serves 4.

> **MAKE IT A PARTY!**
> Choose your linens, dishes and serving utensils days ahead of time. Keep the hues all in the same color tones and your buffet table will look professional!

Pumpkin Joes

Devilish Dinner Rolls

Add little raisins for eyes on the dough before baking to look like ghosts.

$4\frac{1}{2}$ t. active dry yeast
$\frac{1}{2}$ c. warm water, 110 to
    115 degrees
2 c. warm milk, 110 to
    115 degrees
6 T. shortening
2 eggs, beaten
$\frac{1}{4}$ c. sugar
$1\frac{1}{2}$ t. salt
7 to $7\frac{1}{2}$ c. all-purpose flour, divided

In a large bowl, dissolve yeast in warm water. Add warm milk, shortening, eggs, sugar, salt and 3 cups flour. Beat until smooth. Stir in enough of remaining flour to form a soft dough. Turn onto a floured surface; knead until smooth and elastic, 6 to 8 minutes. Dough will be sticky. Place in a greased bowl; turn once to grease top. Cover; let rise in a warm place until double in size, about one hour. Punch down dough; turn onto a lightly floured surface. Divide into 24 pieces; form each into a roll. Arrange on greased baking sheets, 2 inches apart. Cover and let rise until double in bulk, about 30 minutes. Bake at 350 degrees for 20 to 25 minutes, until golden. Remove to wire racks to cool. Makes 2 dozen.

Pumpkin Joes

These hearty Halloween treats fill your guests up fast!

$1\frac{1}{2}$ lbs. ground beef
1 onion, chopped
12-oz. bottle chili sauce
$\frac{1}{2}$ c. canned pumpkin
$10\frac{3}{4}$ oz. can tomato soup
1 T. pumpkin pie spice
1 t. salt
1 t. pepper
6 to 8 hamburger buns

Brown beef with onion in a skillet over medium heat. Drain; stir in remaining ingredients. Reduce heat; cover and simmer, stirring occasionally, for one hour. Serves 6 to 8.

Gobble-It-Up Party Loaf

It's impossible to stop nibbling on warm pieces of this cheesy, oniony bread...yum!

1 round loaf sourdough bread
1 lb. Monterey Jack cheese, sliced
½ c. butter, melted
½ c. green onion, chopped
2 to 3 t. poppy seed

Score bread lengthwise and crosswise without cutting through the bottom. Insert cheese slices between cuts. Combine remaining ingredients; drizzle over bread. Wrap loaf in aluminum foil; place on an ungreased baking sheet. Bake at 350 degrees for 15 minutes. Unwrap loaf and return to oven. Bake an additional 10 minutes, uncovered, until cheese is melted. Serves 10 to 15.

Spicy-Sweet Pumpkin Pie Dip

This dip is perfect for the sweet-tooth at your party!

2 8-oz. pkgs. cream cheese, softened
4 c. powdered sugar
15-oz. can pumpkin
2 t. cinnamon
1 t. ground ginger
gingersnaps, vanilla wafers, graham crackers

Mix together cream cheese and powdered sugar in a large bowl until well blended. Add remaining ingredients except cookies; mix well. Cover and refrigerate. Serve with gingersnaps, vanilla wafers or graham crackers. Serves 12 to 16.

Gobble-It-Up
Party Loaf

Bobbing Apple
Dumplings

Bobbing Apple Dumplings

Apple dumplings are a must during the fall season! If you can make a trip to the orchard, fresh-picked apples just can't be beat.

8-oz. tube refrigerated crescent rolls
2 Granny Smith apples, peeled, cored and
    quartered
$\frac{1}{8}$ t. cinnamon
$\frac{1}{2}$ c. butter
1 c. sugar
1 c. orange juice
1 t. vanilla extract
$\frac{1}{2}$ c. pecans, very finely chopped
Optional: ice cream

Unroll and separate crescent roll dough into triangles. Wrap each piece of apple in a crescent roll. Arrange in a greased 8"x8" baking pan; sprinkle with cinnamon. Combine butter, sugar and orange juice in a medium saucepan. Bring to a boil; remove from heat and stir in vanilla. Pour mixture over dumplings; sprinkle pecans over top. Bake at 350 degrees for 30 minutes, or until crust is golden and beginning to bubble. To serve, spoon some of the syrup from the baking pan over dumplings. Serve with ice cream, if desired. Serves 8.

MAKE IT A PARTY!
Match this yummy treat by bobbing for some real apples! Use a low plastic or metal container, fill with water and then add the apples and watch the fun!

Fiendish Spinach Dip

Surround this yummy dip with veggies that are colorful and fun. . .just like your party!

3 to 4 green onions
$\frac{1}{2}$ c. fresh parsley
10-oz. pkg. frozen chopped spinach, slightly
   thawed
8-oz. pkg. cream cheese, softened
3 T. dried, minced onion
1 c. cottage cheese
1 c. mayonnaise
$\frac{1}{2}$ c. sour cream
$\frac{1}{4}$ t. hot pepper sauce
$\frac{1}{4}$ t. pepper
$\frac{1}{4}$ c. lemon juice
assorted crackers, cut-up vegetables

Combine green onions and parsley in a food processor; pulse to chop. Add spinach and continue to process until spinach has been finely chopped. Remove from processor and set aside. Without rinsing the processor, add remaining ingredients except crackers and vegetables. Blend until well mixed. Stir into spinach mixture, blending well. Spoon into a serving bowl; chill several hours before serving. Serve with crackers and vegetables. Makes about 8 cups.

Fiendish
Spinach Dip

Apricot-Apple Harvest Brew

A cup of this brew is just the potion for a cold Halloween night.

1 gal. apple cider
$11\frac{1}{2}$ oz. can apricot nectar
1 c. sugar
2 c. orange juice
$\frac{3}{4}$ c. lemon juice
4 4-inch cinnamon sticks
2 t. allspice
1 t. ground cloves
$\frac{1}{2}$ t. nutmeg

Bring all ingredients to a boil in a large stockpot over medium heat. Reduce heat; simmer for about 10 minutes. Serves about 20.

Apricot-Apple
Harvest Brew

TRICK OR TREAT!

Here's a Treat:
For a special treat, cut a marshmallow into the shape of a ghost and float in the brew.

Boo-tiful
Pumpkin Cake

Boo-tiful
Pumpkin Cake

Make two recipes of this pumpkin cake and create your own tasty pumpkin!

4 eggs, beaten
2 c. sugar
1 c. oil
15-oz. can pumpkin
2 c. all-purpose flour
1 t. salt
2 t. baking soda
$1\frac{1}{2}$ t. cinnamon

Combine eggs, sugar and oil in a large bowl; beat with an electric mixer on high speed until mixture is lemon-colored and thick. Blend in pumpkin; set aside. In another bowl, whisk together flour, salt, baking soda and cinnamon. Add $\frac{1}{2}$ cup at a time to the pumpkin mixture, blending well after each addition. Pour batter into a lightly greased 13"x9" baking pan and bake at 350 degrees for 40 minutes, or until a toothpick comes out clean. If using a Bundt® pan, bake for 30 minutes at 350 degrees, then reduce temperature to 325 degrees for an additional 20 to 25 minutes. Check for doneness. Cool completely before frosting. Serves 8 to 10.

To make the pumpkin cake shown, prepare the recipe twice, making 2 cakes. Invert one on top of the other. Prepare Cream Cheese Frosting reserving $\frac{1}{2}$ cup for stem. Tint frosting with orange food coloring. Drizzle over cakes. Tint remaining frosting green. Frost an ice cream cone with green frosting and invert for the stem. Sprinkle with edible glitter.

Cream Cheese Frosting:

8-oz. pkg. cream cheese, softened
$\frac{1}{4}$ c. butter, softened
1 t. vanilla extract
$1\frac{1}{2}$ to 2 c. powdered sugar
2 to 3 T. milk

Blend together cream cheese, butter and vanilla. Stir in as much powdered sugar and milk as needed to achieve desired consistency.

MAKE IT A PARTY!

It takes extra time to make a decorated cake for that special party. So after the cake is done, take the time to make a special presentation. Using a cake stand is a fast and easy way to present your cake. There are a variety of cake stands available at retail stores. But don't overlook searching for the perfect dish at flea markets and vintage stores. You might just find the color and style that fits your cake masterpiece!

Lizard Pumpkin Pie

¼ c. plus 2 T. caramel ice cream topping, divided
9-inch graham cracker crust
½ c. plus 2 T. pecan pieces, divided
1 c. milk
2 3.4-oz. pkgs. instant vanilla pudding mix
1 c. canned pumpkin
1 t. cinnamon
½ t. nutmeg
8-oz. container frozen whipped topping, thawed and divided

Pour ¼ cup caramel topping into crust; sprinkle with ½ cup nuts. Beat milk, dry pudding mixes, pumpkin and spices with a whisk until blended. Stir in 1½ cups whipped topping; spread mixture into crust. Refrigerate at least one hour. Before serving, spread pie with remaining whipped topping, drizzle with remaining caramel topping and sprinkle with remaining pecans if desired. Serves 10.

So-Scary Eggnog

Serve this eggnog with just a dusting of nutmeg and orange sugar on top.

½ gal. milk, divided
3.4-oz. pkg. instant vanilla pudding mix
¼ c. sugar
2 t. vanilla extract
½ t. cinnamon
½ t. nutmeg

In a large bowl or pitcher, whisk together ¾ cup milk and pudding mix until smooth. Whisk in sugar, vanilla and spices until sugar dissolves; stir in remaining milk. Chill before serving. Serves 16.

TRICK OR TREAT!

Here's a Trick:
To make the top of the pie artistic, drizzle the caramel one way across the pie. Then use a knife and gently make cutting lines across it.

Lizard Pumpkin Pie

continued from page 46

Haunted Gingerbread Castle Baking Directions:

1. Enlarge and trace pattern pieces, page 195, and cut out. Trace onto parchment paper, and cover with clear plastic laminate. Set aside.
2. Roll about ¼ of the dough out on a large sheet of parchment paper, sprinkling with additional flour to keep dough from sticking to rolling pin. Roll to about ¼-inch thickness.
3. Place pattern pieces on top of dough, leaving at least ½ inch between them. Cut around the pieces with a sharp knife. Remove excess dough and save to re-roll.
4. Place parchment with dough cutouts on a large flat baking sheet. Bake at 375 degrees for 8 to 10 minutes, until cutouts are firm in center. Remove from oven. Carefully place the pattern pieces back on top of the cutouts and re-trim with a sharp knife. Remove pattern pieces and return cutouts to oven for 2 to 4 more minutes, until edges are lightly browned and gingerbread is dry. Remove parchment with cutouts to a rack or counter to cool. Repeat with remaining dough and scraps until you have all pattern pieces baked.
5. Place the 4 sides of castle on foil-lined baking sheet. Fill window cutouts with crushed red candy. Return to oven for 2 to 3 minutes, until candy is melted. Cool completely on foil before peeling the foil away.

If desired, use extra dough to bake Halloween cutout cookies such as ghosts, Frankenstein, tombstones and cats.

Royal Icing:

3 T. meringue powder
⅓ c. plus 2 T. warm water
4 ½ c. powdered sugar
½ t. cream of tartar

In a medium bowl, combine all ingredients. Beat with an electric mixer on low speed until combined. Beat on high speed for 7 minutes, or until very thick and stiff. Keep covered with plastic wrap when not using. Store in refrigerator.

To Construct Haunted Castle You Will Need:

1 recipe Gingerbread Dough
1 recipe Royal Icing
black and green paste food coloring
1 c. red candies, such as Jolly Rancher
pretzel sticks
small candy-coated chocolates, such as Mini M&M's
4 regular and 4 sugar ice cream cones
vanilla wafer sandwich cookies
1 to 2 cups gel icing
½ pkg. chocolate sandwich cookies
chocolate candy coating discs
chocolate candy sprinkles
tassie cups
disposable decorating bags (coupler and tips)

1. Prepare Royal Icing. Tint about ½ of the icing with black paste food coloring. Place some of the black icing in a disposable decorating bag fitted with coupler and sealed shut with twist ties. Keep icing covered with plastic wrap to prevent drying out.
2. While gingerbread cutouts are flat, decorate the sides of the castle with shutters, door, etc. For shutters, split the wafer cookies with a sharp knife and trim to fit. If desired, decorate cutout cookies with white, black and green icings and decorating sugars or candy. Let icing dry before assembling.

Assembling Directions:

1. Line up 2 of the castle sides around the base so that the wall edges overlap at the corner. Pipe a bead of black icing along all the edges of gingerbread that will touch and press in place. Use heavy mugs or tumblers to hold pieces in place until dry, one to 2 hours. Repeat with remaining sides of castle.

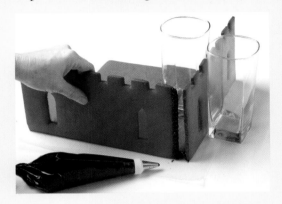

2. Fit together the 2 support pieces and place inside castle. If desired, fill castle with battery operated lights. Place roof piece on top of support pieces.

3. Cut about one inch off the bottoms of the regular ice cream cones. Pipe some white or colored icing inside the cones. Invert the sugar cones and place one sugar cone inside each of the regular cones with icing. Arrange the 4 cone towers on top of castle and secure with some piped icing. Attach small candy-coated chocolates to tops of towers.

4. Split and remove filling from chocolate cookies. Crush the cookies. Sprinkle around the castle. Tint the gel icing green. Spread around the castle for a moat. Arrange decorated cookies on or around castle.

5. For trees, melt chocolate candy coating. Place in a decorating bag and snip end. Pipe melted chocolate trees onto waxed paper. Sprinkle with chocolate candy sprinkles. Cool or chill until set. To stand up, fill several tassie cups with melted chocolate. Peel a chocolate tree from waxed paper and insert base into a cup with melted chocolate. Place in refrigerator or freezer, with support, for a few minutes or until base is hardened.

Note: Castle will keep for several weeks in cool, dry weather.

Sinfully Sensational
Soup Supper

Get ready for a cozy, spooky night of fun and fright. Serve a variety of soup concoctions paired up with tasty quick breads, cheese dips and desserts. So open the door and let the spirited guests arrive…ready to gobble up your Halloween treats.

Getting Ready for the Party:
Plan how you want to present your soups, chowders and breads, and gather the equipment you'll need. If you use slow cookers, be sure you have plenty on hand or borrow from friends.

Party Activities:
Play some old-fashioned Halloween games at this cozy party. One old-time favorite is the doughnut game. Tie strings around doughnuts and hang them from the ceiling. Divide guests into teams. Each team member, with hands tied behind their back, tries to take a bite from the doughnut. The team that wins gets a dozen doughnuts!

The Invitation:
Send an invitation that bubbles over with Halloween fun. The paper cauldron is cut from black scrapbook paper and centered on green cardstock. The little circles become 3-D with a foam dot behind them. Instructions for making the invitation are on page 177. The pattern is on page 193.

Tablescapes:
Make clever name cards using the cauldron pattern from the invitation. Set up the soup supper as a buffet with slow cookers and soup tureens filled with the warm concoctions. Place mismatched spoons in a fruit jar and stack bowls of different fall colors on the buffet. Choose autumn hues in green, creamy white, mustard and brown.

"Anyone who tells a lie has not a pure heart and cannot make a good soup."

— LUDWIG VAN BEETHOVEN

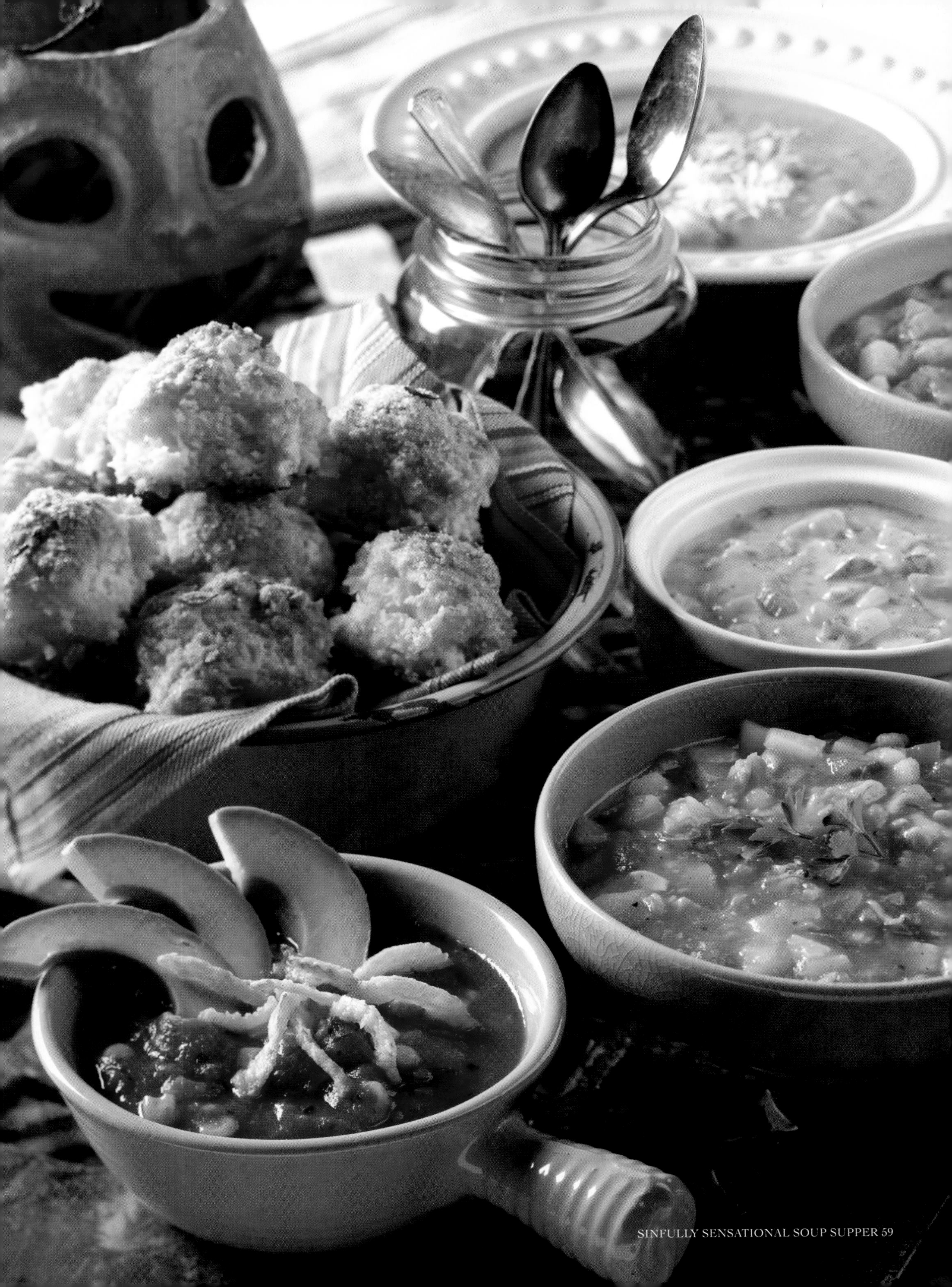

Clammy
Clam Chowder

Clammy
Clam Chowder

Bits of clams and diced tomatoes combine with old-fashioned salt pork to make a soup that will take the chill out of your bones!

4 c. potatoes, peeled and finely diced
1 c. onion, finely diced
2½ c. water
¾ c. salt pork, finely diced
¼ t. seasoned salt
3 c. tomatoes, finely diced
salt and pepper to taste
3 8-oz. cans minced clams, drained

Combine potatoes, onion and water in a large, heavy saucepan over medium heat. Meanwhile, in a skillet over medium-low heat, cook salt pork until drippings have cooked out, being careful not to burn. Add salt pork, drippings and seasoned salt to potato mixture. Simmer until vegetables are tender. Stir in tomatoes; cook 3 to 5 minutes. Add salt and pepper, as desired. Add clams and simmer until heated through; do not boil. Serves 6 to 8.

Slow-Cooked
Veggie-Beef Soup

This favorite soup is easy to make using frozen vegetables. Make it the day before your party and keep refrigerated until party time. The flavors will blend and taste even better!

1 to 1½ lbs. stew beef, cubed
46-oz. can cocktail vegetable juice
2 c. water
5 cubes beef bouillon
½ onion, chopped
2 to 3 potatoes, peeled and cubed
3 c. cabbage, shredded
16-oz. pkg. frozen mixed vegetables

Place all ingredients in a large slow cooker. Cover and cook on low setting for about 9 hours, until all ingredients are tender. Serves 10 to 12.

Teeth & Tongues Soup

Rich and hearty...a meal in itself!

½ lb. stew beef, cubed
1 onion, chopped
8-oz. pkg. sliced mushrooms
1 T. olive oil
4 14½-oz. cans beef broth
¾ c. quick-cooking pearled barley, uncooked

Combine beef, onion, mushrooms and oil in a large saucepan. Cook over medium-high heat for about 10 minutes, or until beef is browned. Stir in broth; bring to a boil. Add barley. Reduce heat and simmer, covered, for 30 to 45 minutes, until beef and barley are tender. Serves 4 to 6.

Mini Cheddar Tombstones

Slices of this easy-to-make bread will look like mini tombstones on your buffet table.

2½ c. shredded Cheddar cheese
3½ c. biscuit baking mix
2 eggs, beaten
1¼ c. milk

Combine cheese and biscuit mix in a large bowl. In a separate bowl, beat together eggs and milk; stir into cheese mixture. Pour into 2 greased 7"x4" loaf pans. Bake at 350 degrees for 40 to 55 minutes. Check for doneness after 40 minutes by inserting a toothpick near center. If not done, bake an additional 5 minutes and test again. Repeat until done. Makes 2 mini loaves.

Don't Be a Chicken Soup

Guaranteed to chase away the chills! For extra goodness, use homemade chicken broth...you'll need about 10 cups.

1 T. butter
½ c. onion, chopped
½ c. celery, chopped
2 32-oz. containers chicken broth
14½ oz. can chicken broth
1 c. cooked chicken, diced
1 c. carrot, peeled and sliced
2 t. dried parsley
salt and pepper to taste
1½ c. thin egg noodles, uncooked

Melt butter in a stockpot over medium heat. Sauté onion and celery in butter until just tender, about 5 minutes. Pour in broth; add remaining ingredients except noodles. Bring to a boil; stir in noodles. Reduce heat slightly and simmer for 15 to 20 minutes, until noodles are tender. Serves 6.

Don't Be
a Chicken Soup

Body Parts Tomato Soup

The tortellini in this soup looks almost like floating body parts…at least it does on Halloween!

12-oz. pkg. frozen cheese tortellini, uncooked
28-oz. can crushed tomatoes
28-oz. can Italian-style diced tomatoes
6-oz. can tomato paste
2 c. half-and-half
1 c. milk
1 t. kosher salt
1 T. pepper, or to taste
Garnish: grated Parmesan cheese

Fill a stockpot with water; bring to a boil over medium-high heat. Add tortellini; return to a boil. Remove from heat and let stand until tortellini float, 15 to 20 minutes; drain. Meanwhile, in a separate stockpot, combine remaining ingredients except garnish; bring to a simmer. Add cooked tortellini; stir. Garnish with Parmesan cheese. Serves 3 to 4.

Chill-to-the-Bone Chili

This chili will actually warm you to the bone! Made in a slow cooker…what could be easier?

1 lb. ground beef, browned and drained
2 28-oz. cans crushed tomatoes
2 15½-oz. cans light red kidney beans
3 T. dried, minced onion
1 T. chili powder
1 T. sugar or to taste
salt and pepper to taste

Place all ingredients in a slow cooker. Cover and cook on high setting for 4 hours. Serves 6.

TRICK OR TREAT!

Here's a Trick:
Want a fun way to present a soup on the buffet? Try putting the soup in a cast iron skillet….it will look very dark and Halloween-like and keep the soup nice and warm.

Creepy Corn Chowder

Thick and rich…this chowder will be gobbled up in no time!

6 slices bacon, finely diced
1 stalk celery, thinly sliced
1 onion, diced
1 redskin potato, diced
¼ c. all-purpose flour
1 T. butter
2 c. whole milk
1½ c. chicken broth
2 c. frozen corn
¾ t. salt
½ t. pepper
½ t. dried sage
½ t. dried thyme
¼ t. celery salt
¼ t. nutmeg
⅛ t. cayenne pepper

Sauté bacon in a Dutch oven or stockpot over medium heat. Add celery, onion and potato. Cook until potato starts to turn golden, about 5 to 7 minutes; drain. Stir in flour and butter. Cook just until mixture starts to bubble, about 3 to 5 minutes. Add remaining ingredients and bring to a boil. Reduce heat and cover. Simmer for 20 to 30 minutes, stirring 2 to 3 times, until potato is tender and chowder has thickened. Serves 4 to 6.

Witch's Wild Rice Potion

Cook the rice the day before to make this soup easy to put together the day of the party. Everyone will say it is howling good!

6-oz. pkg. long grain and wild rice mix,
**   uncooked**
1 lb. ground beef
14½-oz. can chicken broth
10¾-oz. can cream of mushroom soup
2 c. milk
1 c. shredded Cheddar cheese
⅓ c. carrot, peeled and shredded
1-oz. pkg. ranch salad dressing mix
Garnish: chopped green onions

Prepare rice mix according to package directions. Measure out 1½ cups cooked rice and set aside, reserving the remainder for another use. Meanwhile, in a Dutch oven over medium heat, brown beef. Drain; stir in cooked rice and remaining ingredients except garnish. Reduce heat to low and simmer for 15 to 20 minutes, stirring often. Sprinkle servings with green onions. Serves 6 to 8.

Creepy
Corn Chowder

Ghoulish Chowder

What are those things floating in my bowl? Oh, they're only French fried onions, but they do look like something spooky…a spider perhaps?

1 T. butter
2 t. garlic, minced
4 tomatoes, chopped
1 c. water
15-oz. can tomato sauce
1 c. frozen corn
¼ c. fresh cilantro, chopped
1 T. hot pepper sauce
½ t. chili powder
Garnish: avocado slices, shredded Monterey
   Jack cheese, French fried onions

Melt butter in a saucepan over medium heat. Add garlic; cook and stir for one minute. Stir in tomatoes and cook for 5 minutes. Add remaining ingredients except garnish, and bring to a boil. Reduce heat and simmer for 10 minutes. Ladle soup into bowls; garnish as desired. Serves 4.

Ghoulish Chowder

Apple-Cheese Biscuits

Apple-Cheese Biscuits

Take advantage of the local apples this time of year to make these delightfully light biscuits. They are a perfect companion to most any soup!

⅓ c. sugar
⅓ c. sweetened flaked coconut
½ t. cinnamon
3 T. butter or margarine, melted
1¾ c. biscuit baking mix
¾ c. shredded Cheddar cheese
1 tart apple, peeled, cored
  and diced
⅓ c. plus 1 T. milk

Stir together sugar, coconut and cinnamon in a cup. Place butter or margarine in another cup; set aside. In a medium bowl, stir together biscuit mix, cheese and apple; make a well in the center. Add milk all at once, stirring just until dough holds together. Form dough into 16 balls. Dip in butter or margarine; roll in sugar mixture. Arrange in a greased 9" round baking pan. Bake at 400 degrees for about 25 minutes. Serves 16.

Monster-Face Muffins

Adding a few frightening features to these easy-to-make muffins will bring smiles to your party guests.

1 c. cornmeal
1 c. all-purpose flour
½ c. sugar
2½ t. baking powder
¼ t. salt
1 c. buttermilk
½ c. butter, softened
1 egg, beaten
Garnish: sliced olives, green pepper strips

Mix dry ingredients in a large bowl; set aside. Combine remaining ingredients in a separate bowl; add to dry ingredients. Stir until moistened. Divide batter evenly into 12 lightly greased muffin cups. Add olives and pepper strips to make monster faces. Bake at 400 degrees for 15 to 20 minutes. Makes one dozen.

Monster-Face
Muffins

MAKE IT A PARTY!
Serve some savory butters with your cornbread. Fill tiny crocks with chive butter or parsley butter. Simply chop the herb and add it to soft butter. Your guests will love it!

Maple-Brown Sugar Apple Crumble

The smell of this apple dessert in the oven will put you in the mood for leaf raking, pumpkin carving and all your other favorite fall activities.

5 apples, peeled, cored and sliced
⅔ c. maple syrup
½ c. butter, softened
½ c. brown sugar, packed
¾ c. all-purpose flour
¾ c. long-cooking oats, uncooked
⅛ t. salt

Place sliced apples in a lightly greased 8"x 8" baking pan; drizzle maple syrup over apples. In a bowl, blend together butter and brown sugar. Stir in flour, oats and salt until crumbly. Sprinkle butter mixture over apples. Bake, uncovered, at 375 degrees for 35 minutes, or until golden and apples are tender. Serves 4.

Mummified Cheese Log

Shaping this log into a mummy is half the fun. Let the kids help decide how they want this cheesy mummy to look and then start sculpting!

¼ c. chopped pecans
8-oz. pkg. light cream cheese, softened
⅓ c. green onions, chopped
1 t. mustard
1 clove garlic, minced
¼ t. hot pepper sauce
1 c. shredded sharp Cheddar cheese
¼ c. fresh parsley, finely chopped
assorted crackers

Place pecans on an ungreased baking sheet. Bake at 350 degrees for 8 minutes, stirring twice; let cool. Place cream cheese, onions, mustard, garlic and hot pepper sauce in a bowl. Beat with an electric mixer on slow speed for about 3 minutes. Stir in Cheddar cheese. Form into a mummy-shaped log and wrap in plastic wrap. Chill for 15 to 20 minutes. Mix parsley with toasted pecans and spread on a baking sheet or wax paper. Unwrap log and roll in parsley mixture, covering completely. Wrap again in plastic wrap and store in refrigerator until ready to serve. Serve with crackers. Serves 6 to 8.

Halloween Orange Iced Tea

6 c. water
8 teabags
¼ c. fresh mint, chopped
3 T. sugar
2 c. orange juice
juice of 2 lemons
ice

Bring water to a boil in a saucepan. Remove from heat and add teabags, mint and sugar; steep for 20 minutes. Discard teabags, strain out mint. Chill for at least 2 hours. Pour into a large pitcher; add juices. Serve in tall glasses over ice. Serves 6 to 8.

Mummified Cheese Log

Little Monster Bash

Not so scary, but oh so fun, this party is for the littlest of Halloween lovers. Monsters or not, invite all the little ones you know to enjoy this party full of Halloween treats. Kitty Cat Sandwiches, Monsterously Good Cookies and Bewitching Cupcakes combine with corn dogs, veggie pizza and marshmallow bars to make a party to tempt any little ghoul or boy.

Getting Ready for the Party:
Kid parties are always high-energy, so get ready by having all of the goodies on trays ready to serve. Plan where kids can toss their coats or place their shoes so the party gets off to a good start.

Party Activities:
Make a memory by photographing each guest in his or her costume. Print the photos before the kids leave (ask a mom to help) and glue the photo to a prefolded piece of colorful cardstock for a card they'll love to share. Set out the crayons or markers and have the kids decorate the front of their costumed self-portrait cards.

The Invitation:
A one-eyed monster with a happy smile will greet your little party goer when they open their invitation. A fun googly eye and a piece of string makes the invite 3-D. And don't forget to decorate the envelope as well. Instructions for making the invitation are on page 178. The pattern is on page 192.

Tablescapes:
Choose kid-friendly colors such as apple green, bright orange and purple. Keep it simple with polka-dot or striped napkins and orange plastic tableware. A balloon bouquet using the same colors can serve as the centerpiece. Let each guest color on a paper tablecloth. Then sit back and enjoy the fun!

"Once in a young lifetime one should be allowed to have as much sweetness as one can possibly want and hold."

— JUDITH OLNEY

Bewitching Cupcakes

Jack-'O-Lantern Sandwiches

Plain-Jane bagels turn into Jack-'O- Lanterns with just a little green pepper and some bacon strips.

1 c. mayonnaise
1 c. deli ham, chopped
1 c. shredded Cheddar cheese
1 green onion, finely chopped
3 to 4 bagels, halved
3 slices bacon, crisply cooked
green pepper cut into small triangles

In a bowl, combine mayonnaise, ham, cheese and green onion. Spread mixture onto the cut sides of bagel halves. Arrange bagels on a broiler pan. Broil for 5 minutes, until cheese is melted and bubbly. Add cut pieces of green pepper for eyes and a bacon strip for mouth. Serves 3 to 4.

TRICK OR TREAT!

Here's a Trick:
Healthy food can be disguised as part of the party when you add garnishes like sliced apples, carrot strips, sweet peppers and other fresh veggies.

Little Monster Bear Munchies

Little party goers will gobble up this cute little snack!

3-oz. pkg. ramen noodles, uncooked
5 c. bite-size sweetened graham cereal squares
3 c. bear-shaped graham crackers
1 c. dry-roasted peanuts
1 c. raisins
⅓ c. butter
⅓ c. honey
1 t. orange juice
½ t. cinnamon

Crush ramen noodles; reserve seasoning packet for another use. In a large bowl, toss together noodles, cereal, crackers, peanuts and raisins; set aside. Combine remaining ingredients in a microwave-safe cup. Microwave on high, stirring after 15-second intervals, until well mixed and butter is melted. Pour over noodle mixture; toss to coat well. Spread onto ungreased rimmed baking sheets. Bake at 375 degrees for 10 minutes, stirring once. Cool before serving; store in an airtight container. Serves 15.

Kitty Cat Sandwiches

Surprise the kids with these tasty little Halloween cats.

1 egg, beaten
1 T. milk
½ t. cinnamon
1 t. sugar
2 slices white bread
2 t. favorite-flavor jam or jelly
2 t. butter
Garnish: green candies

Whisk together egg, milk, cinnamon and sugar in a bowl. Make a sandwich with bread slices and jam or jelly. Cut with cat cookie cutter. Dip both sides into egg mixture. In a skillet over medium heat, fry in butter until golden on both sides. Add green candies for eyes. Serves one.

Kitty Cat Sandwiches

Goblin's Favorite Corn Dogs

Goblin's Favorite Corn Dogs

Add a little orange food coloring to the batter to make these treats even more Halloween-like.

16-oz. pkg. hot dogs, cut in half
1 c. yellow cornmeal
1 c. all-purpose flour
½ c. sugar
4 t. baking powder
2 t. salt
1 egg, beaten
1 c. milk
oil for deep frying
Optional: orange food coloring, wooden sticks
Garnish: mustard, catsup

Pat hot dogs dry with a paper towel; set aside. In a bowl, stir together cornmeal, flour, sugar, baking powder and salt. Add egg and milk; beat until smooth. Add orange food coloring if desired. In a deep saucepan, heat several inches of oil to 375 degrees. Dip hot dogs in batter and add to oil, several at a time. Keep turning hot dogs until golden on all sides. Place on paper towels to drain. If desired, insert wooden sticks. Serve with mustard and catsup. Serves 8 to 10.

Taffy Apple Pizza

This sweet pizza will be a hit at the party!

18-oz. pkg. refrigerated sugar cookie dough
8-oz. pkg. cream cheese, softened
½ c. brown sugar, packed
¼ c. creamy or crunchy peanut butter
1 t. vanilla extract
2 Granny Smith apples, peeled, cored and sliced
¼ c. caramel ice cream topping
½ c. chopped peanuts

Sticks & Bones

Form cookie dough into a ball and place in the center of a greased 14" round pizza pan. Using a lightly floured rolling pin, roll out to a 14-inch circle, about ¼-inch thick. Bake at 350 degrees for 16 to 18 minutes, until lightly golden. Remove from oven; cool 10 minutes. Loosen cookie from pan slightly with a serrated knife. Combine cream cheese, brown sugar, peanut butter and vanilla; mix well and spread evenly over cookie. Cut apple slices in half and arrange evenly over cream cheese mixture. Microwave topping on high setting for 30 to 45 seconds, until warm; drizzle evenly over apples. Sprinkle peanuts over top; cut into wedges. Serves 8 to 10.

Sticks & Bones

These fries are yummy and nutritious!

**2-lb. butternut squash, halved lengthwise,
    seeded and peeled**
2 t. olive oil
salt to taste
½ t. ground cumin
½ t. chili powder
½ c. sour cream
2 T. maple syrup

Cut squash halves to resemble French fries; slice about ½-inch wide and 3 inches long. Add oil to a large bowl; add squash, tossing to coat. Line a baking sheet with aluminum foil; spray with non-stick vegetable spray. Arrange slices in a single layer on top. Bake at 425 degrees for 35 minutes, or until tender. Combine salt, cumin and chili powder; sprinkle desired amount over fries. Blend together sour cream and syrup as a dipping sauce. Serves 4.

Chewy Gumdrop Cookies

Little gumdrops add color and sweetness to this party treat.

1 c. shortening
1 c. sugar
½ c. brown sugar, packed
2 eggs, beaten
1 t. vanilla extract
2⅓ c. all-purpose flour
1 t. baking soda
1 t. salt
1 c. gumdrops, chopped
Optional: ½ c. chopped nuts

In a large bowl, blend together shortening, sugars, eggs and vanilla. Add flour, baking soda and salt. Fold in gumdrops and nuts, if desired. Mix well. Drop by teaspoonfuls onto ungreased baking sheets. Bake at 350 degrees for 15 minutes. Makes about 4 dozen.

Chewy Gumdrop Cookies

Bewitching Cupcakes

These little cupcakes are bewitched indeed! You really do frost them before baking! Adding the little character on top is just the icing on the cake!

⅓ c. shortening
1 c. sugar
2 eggs, separated
½ c. milk
1 t. vanilla extract
1⅔ c. all-purpose flour
2 t. baking powder
½ t. salt
½ c. brown sugar, packed
2 T. baking cocoa
¼ c. chopped pecans

Combine shortening and sugar; blend until smooth. Add one egg plus one yolk, milk and vanilla. Sift together flour, baking powder and salt; stir into shortening mixture until smooth. Fill paper-lined muffin cups ½ full; set aside. Beat remaining egg white with an electric mixer at high speed until stiff peaks form. Add brown sugar and cocoa; beat until well blended. Spoon a generous teaspoonful over each cupcake; sprinkle with nuts. Bake at 350 degrees for 20 minutes. After baking, color in Halloween Cake Pokes, adhere toothpick to the back and place in cupcakes. Makes 12 to 15.

Note: For patterns for the Halloween Cake Pokes, see page 204.

Bewitching Cupcakes

Sloppy Goblins

Sloppy Goblins

With only 5 ingredients, these yummy Sloppy Goblins couldn't be easier!

1 lb. ground beef
½ c. onion, diced
10¾-oz. can chicken gumbo soup
3 T. catsup
1 T. mustard
8 hamburger buns, split and toasted

Brown beef and onion in a skillet over medium heat; drain. Stir in soup, catsup and mustard. Simmer 30 minutes; spoon onto warm buns. Serves 8.

MAKE IT A PARTY!

Have a simple costume judging at the party. Make up categories such as "funniest" costume, "most colorful costume" or "most original costume." Be sure there are enough categories so everyone wins a prize!

Vampire's Veggie Pizza

Everyone will want to take a bite out of this yummy pizza. Cut the pizza into bite-size squares for easy nibbling.

2 8-oz. tubes refrigerated crescent rolls
8-oz. pkg. cream cheese, softened
1-oz. pkg. ranch salad dressing mix
1 c. broccoli, finely chopped
1 c. carrot, shredded
1 c. green peppers, diced or cut into shapes
1 c. mini pepperoni
½ c. sliced olives
½ c. celery, chopped
1 to 2 c. shredded Cheddar cheese

Roll out crescent roll dough onto an ungreased baking sheet. Press seams together to form a rectangle. Pinch together edges to form a crust. Bake at 375 degrees for 12 minutes; cool completely. Combine cream cheese and ranch dip. Spread over crust; top with vegetables, then cheese. Cover and refrigerate for at least an hour; cut into squares. Serves 16.

Vampire's Veggie Pizza

Halloween Party Mix

Put this mix into bags, tie with pretty Halloween ribbon and give to little trick-or-treaters.

2 c. candy-coated peanut butter-filled candies
2 c. doughnut-shaped oat cereal
2 c. candy corn
2 c. honeycomb-shaped corn and oat cereal
2 c. salted peanuts
2 c. bagel chips
2 c. bite-size crispy rice cereal squares

Toss all ingredients together. Store in an airtight container. Makes 14 cups.

Forbidden Marshmallow Bars

With so many favorite flavors, these bars are sure to be a hit at the party!

2 eggs, beaten
¾ c. sugar
½ c. butter or margarine
1 t. vanilla extract
2½ c. graham crackers, crushed
½ c. chopped nuts
½ c. sweetened flaked coconut
2½ c. mini marshmallows
11-oz. pkg. butterscotch chips
3 T. creamy peanut butter

In a saucepan over medium-high heat, combine eggs, sugar, butter or margarine and vanilla. Cook until thick; set aside to cool. Stir in graham crackers, nuts, coconut and marshmallows. Mix together well and pat into a greased 13"x9" baking pan. In a separate saucepan over medium heat, stir together butterscotch chips and peanut butter until melted and smooth; spread over bars and set aside to cool. Cut into bars. Makes 1½ dozen.

Witches' Brew

Scare them silly by floating a frozen hand in this yummy brew!

6-oz. pkg. cherry gelatin mix
2 c. sugar
4 c. boiling water
¾ c. frozen lemonade concentrate
48-oz. can pineapple juice
4½ c. cold water
1 to 2 2-ltr. bottles lemon-lime soda, chilled

Stir gelatin mix and sugar into boiling water until completely dissolved. Add lemonade and pineapple juice; mix well. Blend in cold water. Pour mixture into gallon-size plastic freezer bags; freeze overnight. Remove bags from the freezer 2 hours before serving; knead slightly while in bag. Place mixture in a punch bowl, adding desired amount of soda. Serves 45.

To make the floating hand, rinse out a disposable plastic glove. Fill with water that has been colored with green food coloring. Freeze until firm. Remove glove by running cold water over the glove. Cut away some of the plastic glove and gently remove hand. Float ice hand in punch bowl.

MAKE IT A PARTY!
Be sure to have plenty of activities for the kids at the party. Reading Halloween stories or poems is a fun way to settle down the crowd for a few minutes. Then try a variation of a favorite party game. Play "Pin the Face on the Pumpkin." Simply cut out a large pumpkin shape and take turns pinning face shapes on the paper. . .blindfolded, of course!

Monstrously
Good Cookies

Monstrously
Good Cookies

*This recipe is designed to make enough cookies for
all the trick-or-treaters on the block...with plenty left
over for the entire family as well!*

2 c. butter or margarine, softened
6¼ c. crunchy peanut butter
2 16-oz. pkgs. brown sugar
4 c. sugar
1 T. corn syrup
1 T. vanilla extract
8 t. baking soda

1 doz. eggs, beaten
12-oz. pkg. chocolate chips
16-oz. pkg. candy-coated chocolates or candy-
    coated peanut butter-filled candies
18 c. quick-cooking oats, uncooked

In a very large bowl, mix together ingredients
in order given. Place dough by ¼ cupfuls on
ungreased baking sheets. Bake at 350 degrees
for 8 to 10 minutes. Makes 12 dozen.

Wormy Popcorn Balls

Add a gummy worm to this little treat for some Halloween fun.

20 c. popped popcorn
2 c. sugar
½ c. water
⅔ c. corn syrup
1 t. vanilla extract
1 t. salt
1 c. gummy worm candies

Place popcorn in a large heat-proof bowl; set aside. In a saucepan over medium heat, mix together remaining ingredients except worm candies. Bring to a boil. Stir mixture until it reaches the thread stage, or 230 to 233 degrees on a candy thermometer. Pour over popcorn; mix well and form into balls with well-buttered hands. Poke a hole with finger and add gummy worms. Reform ball as needed. Wrap balls in squares of wax paper. Makes about 10.

Wormy Popcorn Balls

Scary Movie Countdown Party

Set the stage for some Halloween fun by hosting a party complete with "terrorific" desserts to eat while you watch favorite horror movies. Whether you offer a classic chocolate fondue or an entertaining piece of pie…your guests will be spellbound with the choices they have!

Getting Ready for the Party:
Because your party theme is centered around showing horror films, be sure you have plenty of movies for showing. Set up the chairs or movie viewing area so everyone can be equally terrified.

Party Activities:
Get the party rolling with some name tags with horror movie stars names on them. Hand a name tag to each guest when they arrive. Then have everyone guess which movie star was featured in some of the scary movies you watch at the party. Watch all-time favorite horror movies such as *Psycho, Frankenstein's Castle of Freaks, Dracula, The Fly, The Fearless Vampire Killers, The Birds* or *Son of Frankenstein*.

The Invitation:
An all black and white invitation is a fun way to declare that there might be a film night ahead. A filmstrip motif features all kinds of photo images that will scare them silly. The invitation offers a ticket that the guest can bring to the party…to be sure they get in the door! For instructions on how to make the invitation, see page 192.

Tablescapes:
Start with a color scheme of black and white…just like the great old horror films. Then let over-the-top masks and costumes be the inspiration for your table decorations. A Frankenstein mask in the middle of the table or a set of Dracula teeth laying beside the punch bowl is all you need to get this scary party started.

"Acting is like a Halloween mask that you put on."
— RIVER PHOENIX

"I've seen enough **horror movies** to know that any **weirdo** wearing a mask is never friendly."

— FRIDAY THE 13TH PART VI: JASON LIVES (1986)

Dark Soul Fondue

Dutch Apple Crumb Pie

Dutch Apple Crumb Pie

What a great apple pie! Your guests will love munching on this during a scary movie.

8 tart apples, peeled, cored and sliced
1 c. brown sugar, packed and divided
1 to 2 t. cinnamon, to taste
9-inch pie crust
⅓ c. butter, chilled
¾ c. plus 2 T. all-purpose flour, divided
Garnish: whipped cream or ice cream

Toss together apples, ½ cup brown sugar, 2 tablespoons flour and cinnamon. Place apple mixture into pie crust; set aside. In a separate large bowl, combine butter, flour and remaining brown sugar. Using a pastry cutter, work mixture into small crumbs; sprinkle over apples. Bake at 425 degrees for 10 minutes. Reduce oven to 350 degrees and bake an additional 30 to 35 minutes. Cool slightly until just warm. Serve with whipped cream or ice cream. Serves 8.

TRICK OR TREAT!

Here's a Treat:
Serve this yummy apple pie with a scoop of some cinnamon ice cream. Or cut some Cheddar cheese wedges to serve with the pie. Either way, your guests will love it!

Frankenstein's Pistachio Cake

Here is a cake that will make you green with envy if you are not the one eating it!

18½-oz. pkg. yellow or white cake mix
½ c. milk
½ c. water
½ c. oil
5 eggs, beaten
2 3.4-oz. pkgs. instant pistachio pudding mix
Optional: ½ c. chopped nuts

In a large bowl, blend together dry cake mix, milk, water, oil and eggs until smooth. Add dry pudding mix; stir well. Mix in nuts, if using. Pour batter into a lightly greased 13"x9" baking pan. Bake at 325 degrees for 45 minutes. Check for doneness with a toothpick; bake an additional 5 to 10 minutes, if needed. Cool completely; spread Cream Cheese Icing over cooled cake. Serves 12 to 15.

Cream Cheese Icing:

8-oz. pkg. cream cheese, softened
¼ c. butter, softened
1 t. vanilla extract
16-oz. pkg. powdered sugar
3 to 4 T. milk
1 to 2 drops green food coloring
Garnish: ¾ c. chopped nuts

In a large bowl, blend together cream cheese, butter, vanilla and powdered sugar. Add enough milk for a spreadable consistency; stir in food coloring. Garnish with nuts.

MAKE IT A PARTY!
If possible, show the movies on a big screen TV to get the full effect of the film. And be sure to shut off all of the lights when the movie is showing. Light a single candle for just a flicker of light.

Frankenstein's Pistachio Cake

Cheesy Snake Cake

This cheesy cake takes on a scary look when a snake slithers across the top!

18¼ oz. pkg. marble cake mix
32-oz. container ricotta cheese
4 eggs, beaten
¾ c. sugar
1 T. vanilla extract
1 c. milk
3.4-oz. pkg. instant vanilla pudding mix
8-oz. container frozen whipped topping,
　thawed
Snake Decoration:
1 c. plus 3 T. frozen whipped topping,
　thawed and divided
green and yellow food coloring
Garnish: colored sugars, fruit leather

Prepare cake mix according to package directions. Pour batter into a greased and floured 13"x9" baking pan; set aside. In a large bowl, mix together ricotta cheese, eggs, sugar and vanilla. Carefully pour mixture over cake batter; do not stir. Bake at 350 degrees for one hour and 10 minutes. Cool cake completely in pan. In a bowl, whisk together milk and dry pudding mix; fold in whipped topping. Spread over cooled cake. For Snake Decoration, color 1 cup whipped topping with green food coloring. Pipe on top of cake in snake shape. Color 3 tablespoons of whipped topping with yellow food coloring. Pipe two dots for eyes. Add fruit leather tongue. Sprinkle with colored sugars. Refrigerate until ready to serve. Serves 12.

Cheesy Snake Cake

Apparition Apple Cake

Chopped apples and walnuts make the perfect combination for this fall dessert. Add a dollop of whipped cream and dust with a little orange sugar to make this cake even more special!

1½ c. sugar
1 c. all-purpose flour
2 t. baking powder
½ t. salt
2 eggs, beaten
1 t. vanilla extract
2 c. tart apples, cored and chopped
1 c. walnuts, coarsely chopped
Garnish: whipped cream, colored sugar

Blend together sugar, flour, baking powder and salt in a large bowl. Add remaining ingredients except garnish; stir well. Spread in a greased 13"x9" baking pan. Bake, uncovered, at 350 degrees for 30 minutes. Serve topped with dollops of whipped cream. Sprinkle with colored sugar. Serves 12.

Dark Soul Fondue

Dark Soul Fondue

This chocolatey fondue will be a hit at the party. Cut the pound cake into bone shapes or other fun shapes to fit your movie party theme.

¾ c. whipping cream
⅛ t. salt
1 c. milk chocolate chips
1 c. semi-sweet chocolate chips
2½ T. cherry extract
1 T. corn syrup
pound cake cubes, assorted fruit cubes and
    slices

In a saucepan over medium heat, bring cream and salt to a boil. Remove from heat. Add chocolates to saucepan; cover and let stand for a few minutes. Uncover; whisk until smooth. Whisk in extract and corn syrup. Serve immediately with pound cake and fruit. May be kept warm in a slow cooker or fondue pot over low heat; stir often. Serves 10.

Freaky Frothy Pie

So easy and sure to be a favorite!

15-oz. can pumpkin
7-oz. jar marshmallow creme
¼ c. brown sugar, packed
2 t. pumpkin pie spice
12-oz. container frozen whipped topping,
    thawed and divided
9-inch graham cracker pie crust

In a large bowl, whisk together pumpkin, marshmallow creme, brown sugar and spice. Fold in 3½ cups whipped topping; return remaining topping to refrigerator. Spoon pumpkin mixture into crust. Cover and freeze for at least 4 hours, until firm. At serving time, let stand at room temperature for a few minutes before cutting. Garnish with remaining topping. Serves 8.

> **MAKE IT A PARTY!**
> Ask friends to bring fondue pots to share so you can have lots of pots going! If they have vintage fondue pots, that is even more fun. Have the items to be dipped cut and ready to go before the party starts.

Bat Wing
Butterscotch Pie

This pie has a really rich butterscotch flavor. Top each slice with a generous dollop of whipped cream. Then add a sweet bat shape!

1 c. brown sugar, packed
¼ c. butter, softened
¼ c. all-purpose flour
2 c. milk, divided
3 egg yolks, beaten
⅛ t. salt
½ t. vanilla extract
9-inch graham cracker crust
Garnish: whipped cream, caramelized sugar
   bat pieces

In a saucepan over medium-low heat, stir together brown sugar and butter until butter melts and sugar dissolves. Cook 2 to 3 more minutes; remove from heat. In a separate bowl, mix together flour and one cup milk until smooth. Add egg yolks and salt; mix well and stir in remaining milk. Add flour mixture to brown sugar mixture in saucepan. Cook over medium-low heat until thickened, stirring constantly. Remove from heat; stir in vanilla. Spoon filling into crust; chill thoroughly. To make **caramelized sugar bat pieces,** melt ⅓ cup granulated sugar in small saucepan without stirring. Drizzle over a piece of lightly greased aluminum foil. Cool; break into pieces. Top cooled pie with whipped cream and sugar bat pieces. Serves 6 to 8.

Bat Wing Butterscotch Pie

Scissor Fingers Cake

Scissor Fingers Cake

Just a few little almond slices make these ladyfingers have quite the fingernails!

18 to 24 ladyfingers, split and divided
2 1-oz. sqs. unsweetened baking chocolate
½ c. sugar
¼ c. water
4 pasteurized eggs, separated
1 c. butter, softened
2¼ c. powdered sugar
½ t. vanilla extract
Garnish: whipped cream, sliced almonds,
   sprinkles

Line the bottom and sides of an ungreased 9" round springform pan with split ladyfingers, trimming off the bottoms to make ladyfingers stand. Set aside. In a double boiler over medium heat, cook and stir chocolate, sugar and water until chocolate is melted and smooth. In a separate bowl, beat egg yolks and gradually add to chocolate mixture, stirring constantly until smooth; cool. Blend together butter, powdered sugar and vanilla; mix well. Add chocolate mixture; stir well and set aside. With an electric mixer on high speed, beat egg whites until stiff peaks form; fold into chocolate mixture. Spoon mixture into lined pan. Arrange any remaining ladyfingers on top. Top with whipped cream and sprinkles. Refrigerate until ready to serve. To serve, remove outer ring of springform pan. Place cake on cake stand. Use a tiny dot of whipped cream to add a sliced almond to each of the ladyfingers to resemble fingernails. Serves 12.

Terrormisu Toffee Treat

An often-fancy dessert becomes simple when you use purchased pound cake for the base.

10¾-oz. pkg. frozen pound cake, thawed and
   cut into 9 slices
¾ c. strong brewed coffee
1 c. sugar
½ c. chocolate syrup
8-oz. pkg. cream cheese, softened
2 c. whipping cream
2 1.4-oz. chocolate-covered toffee candy bars,
   chopped
Optional: whipped cream, chocolate syrup

Arrange cake slices in the bottom of an ungreased 11"x7" baking pan. Drizzle coffee over cake; set aside. In a large bowl, beat sugar, chocolate syrup and cream cheese with an electric mixer on medium speed until smooth. Add whipping cream; beat on medium speed until light and fluffy. Spread over cake. Sprinkle cake with chopped candy. Cover and refrigerate for one to 8 hours. If desired, garnish portions at serving time with dollops of whipped cream and a drizzle of chocolate syrup. Serves 8.

MAKE IT A PARTY!

If weather permits, move the party outside and show the movie on a homemade screen…a white bedsheet pulled taut on the side of the garage. Put blankets on the lawn and bring the goodies outside to watch the show. The stars above and the night sky might even bring a vision of a witch or two flying above!

Godzilla Cookie

Godzilla Cookie

The movie to watch while you eat this cookie is a no-brainer! Godzilla of course!

2¼ c. all-purpose flour
1 t. baking powder
½ t. salt
1 c. butter, softened
1½ c. brown sugar, packed
1 t. vanilla extract
2 eggs
2 c. semi-sweet chocolate chips

In a small bowl, combine flour, baking powder and salt; set aside. In a large bowl, beat butter, brown sugar and vanilla with an electric mixer on medium speed about 3 to 5 minutes, until mixture is creamy and has turned almost white. Add eggs, one at a time, beating well after each addition. Gradually beat in flour mixture. Stir in chocolate chips. Spread dough evenly onto a parchment paper-lined 14" round pizza pan. Bake at 350 degrees for 30 to 40 minutes, until edges turn golden. Let cool for 10 minutes in pan before removing. Cool completely. Serves 10 to 15.

Cinema-Mocha Mix

*This is great drink when you are shivering from fright!
It warms you to your toes!*

1¾ c. powdered non-dairy creamer
¾ c. sugar
½ c. baking cocoa
⅓ c. instant coffee granules
¼ c. brown sugar, packed
1 t. cinnamon
¼ t. salt
¼ t. nutmeg

Place all ingredients in a blender or food
processor and pulse until finely ground. Store
in an airtight container. To serve, stir ¼ cup mix
into ¾ cup boiling water. Serves 14.

Bloody Thirst Quencher

*Make this cool and welcoming beverage to add some
color to your spooky party!*

3-oz. pkg. cherry gelatin mix
1 c. boiling water
6-oz. can frozen lemonade or pineapple-
   lemonade concentrate
3 c. cold water
32-oz. bottle cranberry juice cocktail
32-oz. bottle ginger ale, chilled

Dissolve gelatin mix in boiling water; stir in
frozen concentrate. Pour into a large pitcher
along with cold water and cranberry juice; chill.
At serving time, slowly add ginger ale. Serves
6 to 8.

Cinema-Mocha Mix

Oh-So-Easy Apple Cider

*Everyone loves a cup of cider…and this one is as pretty
as it is delicious!*

3 qts. apple juice
2 qts. cranberry juice cocktail
½ c. brown sugar, packed
4 4-inch cinnamon sticks

Mix all ingredients together in a large stockpot.
Simmer over low heat until hot; keep warm.
Serves about 40.

Ghostly Cookie Caper

For all of your Halloween-loving friends that like to gobble up cookies, this is the party for them! Rolled, dropped, cut-outs or bars, cookies are the star attraction at this party. The invitation even offers them a cookie cutter and a recipe to get started. Then ask each guest to bring their favorite cookie concoction to share and exchange. It won't be a trick to send each guest home with a plate full of Halloween cookie treats!

you are invited to a **ghostly** cookie caper!

It's a cookie exchange
of the ghostly kind
with the friendliest goblins
you'll ever find!
Wear a Halloween costume
to look your best
and bring 24 cookies to
share with our guests!

Saturday, October 24 • 1-4pm
1313 Black Cat Lane
RSVP to Katie at 555-5555

Getting Ready for the Party:
Be sure you have plenty of fun recipe cards and pens available for writing down those favorite recipes. Offer an array of drinks to serve with the cookies such as coffee, tea, cider and cold milk.

Party Activities:
The activity for this party is to exchange cookies and cookie recipes. Party-goers can write down their favorites. Colorful paper plates can serve as take-home containers…or make some more elaborate containers using paper and stickers.

Tablescapes:
Have the table ready with lots of clear cookie jars or plates to hold the cookies. Hang some cookies on a twig light for a quick and sparkling centerpiece.

The Invitation:
This clever invitation is given or sent in a box that offers not only the written invite, but a cookie cutter, and a special sugar cookie recipe. For instructions on how to make the invitation box, see page 178.

*"A balanced diet is a **cookie** in each hand."*
— ANON

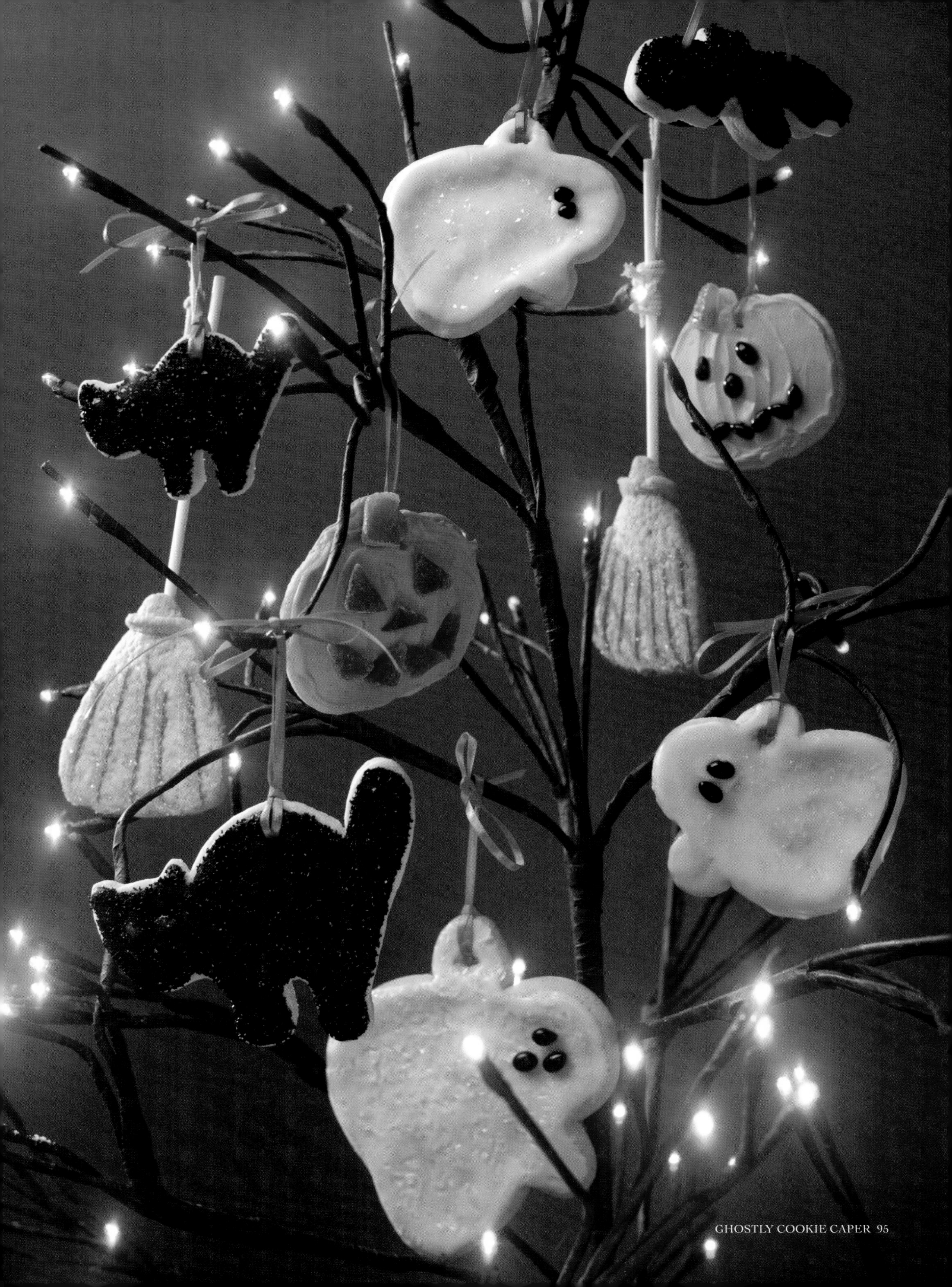

Cookie Bugs

The anise in these little cookies goes well with the little licorice legs on each one!

2 eggs, at room temperature
1 c. sugar
¾ t. anise extract
1 c. all-purpose flour
Garnish: licorice, mini chocolate chips

Place eggs in a large bowl. Beat with an electric mixer on high speed for 4 minutes. Gradually beat in sugar. Continue beating on high speed for 10 minutes, until mixture thickens. Add extract; reduce mixer to low speed and beat in flour. Drop dough by rounded teaspoonfuls onto greased baking sheets. Insert pieces of cut licorice for legs and antennae. Let dry at room temperature, 10 to 12 hours or overnight. Do not refrigerate. Bake on top rack of oven at 350 degrees for 10 to 12 minutes. Remove cookies from baking sheets as soon as they come out of oven. Immediately press in chocolate chip eyes. Makes 2 to 2½ dozen.

Cookie Bugs

Witches' Brooms

Any witch would love to have a sweet broom like these yummy cookies!

1 c. butter or margarine, softened
2 c. brown sugar, packed
2 eggs, beaten
4½ c. all-purpose flour
2 t. baking powder
1 t. baking soda
½ c. milk
1 t. vanilla extract
1 t. lemon extract
lollipop sticks
Garnish: canned frosting, colored sugar

In a large bowl, combine all ingredients except sticks and garnish; mix well. Cover; refrigerate for one hour. Roll out dough ½-inch thick on a floured surface. Cut out triangle shapes. Place on greased and floured cookie sheet with cookie stick tucked underneath. Add strip of dough at top of triangle. Bake at 350 degrees for 10 minutes, or until golden around edges. Cool for one minute before removing from baking sheets; cool completely on wax paper. Pipe cooled cookies with frosting. Sprinkle with orange sugar. Makes about 4 dozen.

Raisin Rocks

These fruit and nut cookies have just the right spice to go with a cup of cider.

1½ c. brown sugar, packed
⅔ c. butter-flavored shortening
2 eggs
1 t. vanilla extract
2½ c. all-purpose flour
1 t. baking soda
¼ t. salt
1 t. cinnamon
¼ t. ground cloves
3 c. chopped pecans
1½ c. raisins

Witches' Brooms

In a large bowl, blend together brown sugar and shortening until light and fluffy. Add eggs one at a time; beat well after each. Stir in vanilla; set aside. In a separate bowl, sift together dry ingredients. Gradually add flour mixture to brown sugar mixture; mix well. Fold in pecans and raisins. Drop by teaspoonfuls onto parchment paper-lined baking sheets. Bake at 325 degrees for 10 to 15 minutes, until golden. Makes 6 dozen.

Goblin Good Orange Cookies

The zest of an orange makes these cookies a Halloween favorite!

1 c. butter, softened
2 c. sugar
2 eggs, beaten
$4\frac{1}{2}$ c. all-purpose flour
1 t. baking powder
1 t. baking soda
1 c. buttermilk
zest and juice of 1 orange
Garnish: candied orange slice

Blend together butter and sugar in a large bowl. Add eggs and beat well. In a separate bowl, sift together flour, baking powder and baking soda. Add flour mixture to butter mixture alternately with buttermilk; mix well. Stir in zest and juice. Drop by tablespoonfuls onto lightly greased baking sheets. Bake at 350 degrees for 8 to 12 minutes. Cool cookies completely before frosting. Spread Orange Frosting on top; garnish with candied orange slice. Makes 4 dozen.

Orange Frosting:

4 c. powdered sugar
2 T. butter, melted
juice of $\frac{1}{2}$ orange
orange food coloring

Blend ingredients together in a small bowl until smooth.

Goblin Good
Orange Cookies

Harvest Moon Cookies

These crunchy almond cookies can be made ahead of time and kept in a cookie tin for several days.

1 lb. butter, softened
1 c. sugar
2 t. vanilla extract
1 c. almonds, finely chopped
3 c. all-purpose flour
Garnish: powdered sugar

Blend together butter and sugar in a large bowl; stir in vanilla and almonds. Gradually add flour until dough can be shaped with your hands. Cover; refrigerate dough for one hour. Form into crescent shapes, about ½-inch thick and 2 inches long. Place on ungreased baking sheets. Bake at 350 degrees for about 15 minutes, or until golden. Remove from oven; cool slightly, then roll in powdered sugar to coat. Store in a covered container. Makes about 3 dozen.

Black Cats & Bats

Don't let these black cats and bats scare you...they are as sweet as can be.

⅔ c. shortening
1½ c. sugar
2 eggs, beaten
1 t. vanilla extract
4 t. milk
3⅓ c. all-purpose flour
2½ t. baking powder
½ t. salt
Garnish: black sanding sugar, green gel icing

In a large bowl, blend shortening and sugar; add eggs, vanilla and milk. In a separate bowl, mix remaining ingredients. Add flour mixture to shortening mixture; stir until well blended.

Divide dough into 3 or 4 balls; wrap in plastic wrap and chill for at least one hour. Roll out dough ¼-inch thick on a floured surface. Cut out shapes with cookie cutters. Transfer to ungreased baking sheets. Bake at 400 degrees for 7 to 9 minutes. Cool before frosting. Tint Powdered Sugar Frosting black, page 104; spread on cookies. Sprinkle with black sanding sugar while still wet. Add eyes with green gel icing. Makes about 3 dozen.

TRICK OR TREAT!

Here's a Trick:
Roll and cut out the shapes of these cookies, bake them days before you are ready to start decorating. Simply freeze them until you have time to do the decorating.

Black Cats & Bats

Haunting Slices

Scary Scotcharoo Bars

So chewy and good, these cookies are perfect for party trays or just for snacking!

1 c. sugar
1 c. light corn syrup
1 c. creamy peanut butter
6 c. crispy rice cereal
1 c. semi-sweet chocolate chips
1 c. butterscotch chips

Combine sugar and corn syrup in a large heavy saucepan. Cook over medium heat, stirring often, until mixture bubbles. Remove from heat; stir in peanut butter and mix well. Add cereal; stir until well coated. Press mixture into a buttered 13"x9" baking pan; set aside. Place chocolate chips and butterscotch chips in a medium saucepan. Cook over low heat until melted; stir until well blended and smooth. Spread chocolate chip mixture over cereal mixture. Cool; cut into squares. Makes 2 dozen.

Haunting Slices

Slicing these cookies is half the fun. You never know what silly or scary expression you will get!

1 c. butter, softened
2 c. brown sugar, packed
2 eggs
1 t. vanilla extract
4 c. all-purpose flour
1 t. baking soda
1 t. cream of tartar
1 c. chopped walnuts
orange food coloring
Garnish: mini chocolate chips

In a large bowl, blend together butter and brown sugar until fluffy. Add eggs, one at a time, mixing thoroughly. Stir in vanilla. Add dry ingredients and nuts; mix well. Take out one cup of dough and tint orange. Form remaining dough into 2 logs, tucking the colored dough in the middle of each log; wrap in wax paper, then in aluminum foil. Refrigerate overnight. Slice dough ¼-inch thick; add chocolate chip eyes. Place on ungreased baking sheets. Bake at 350 degrees for 10 to 12 minutes. Makes about 4 dozen.

Scary Scotcharoo Bars

Spider Spirals

Spider Spirals

Rich and chewy, these little spirals of sweetness will disappear from the cookie tray in no time!

1 c. butter or margarine, softened
2 c. brown sugar, packed
3 eggs, beaten
4 c. all-purpose flour
1 t. baking soda
$\frac{1}{8}$ t. salt

Blend together butter or margarine and brown sugar. Add remaining ingredients; mix well. Cover and chill dough for one hour; divide into 4 parts. Roll out each part $\frac{1}{2}$-inch thick on a floured surface. Spread with Date Filling; roll up jelly-roll fashion. Chill again. Slice $\frac{1}{4}$-inch thick; place on lightly greased baking sheets. Bake at 400 degrees for 12 minutes. Makes 2 dozen.

Date Filling:

1 lb. dates, chopped
$\frac{1}{2}$ c. water
$\frac{1}{2}$ c. sugar
$\frac{1}{2}$ c. black walnuts, chopped

In a saucepan over medium-low heat, combine dates, water and sugar. Cook 5 minutes, stirring frequently. Add walnuts; cool.

Mayhem Molasses Crinkles

Mayhem Molasses Crinkles

This old-time favorite cookie goes great with a hot cup of coffee or tea.

¾ c. shortening
2 c. powdered sugar
1 c. molasses
1 egg, beaten
4 c. all-purpose flour
2 t. baking soda
1 t. salt
1 t. cinnamon
2 t. ground ginger
1 t. vanilla extract
Garnish: sparkling sugar

In a large bowl, blend together shortening, powdered sugar, molasses and egg. Add remaining ingredients except garnish; stir until blended. Roll into one-inch balls, dip in sparkling sugar and place on ungreased baking sheets. Bake at 350 degrees for 10 to 12 minutes, until cookies crack. Cool. Makes 5 dozen.

Pumpkin Family Cut-Outs

This basic sugar cookie recipe lends itself to all kinds of cut-out ideas. Make pumpkin family members with unique personalities by adding candies or cut up pieces of candy to make all kinds of faces.

1 c. shortening
1½ c. sugar
2 eggs, beaten
1 t. vanilla extract
½ c. milk
4 c. all-purpose flour
1½ t. baking soda
1 t. baking powder
½ t. salt
canned frosting
orange food coloring
assorted candies

Blend together shortening and sugar in a large bowl; add eggs and beat well. Add vanilla, milk and dry ingredients; mix together well. Roll out dough ¼-inch to ½-inch thick on a floured surface. Cut out shapes with cookie cutters; transfer to lightly greased baking sheets. Bake at 350 degrees for about 10 minutes, or until cookies are golden on the bottom. Tint canned frosting with orange food coloring. Frost cookies and add faces using candy. Makes 4 to 6 dozen, depending on size of cookie cutters used.

MAKE IT A PARTY!

Have white bakery boxes and cellophane sacks available to decorate for special take-home containers. Just set out stickers, markers, ribbons and crafts glue and let your guests create!

Pumpkin Family Cut-Outs

Ghost-Like Treats

The flavor of these cookies is hauntingly good!

1 c. shortening
2½ c. sugar
3 eggs, beaten
1 t. vanilla extract
4 t. buttermilk
3 c. all-purpose flour
1 t. baking soda
Garnish: sanding sugar, small jellybeans

In a large bowl, blend together shortening and sugar. Add remaining ingredients; beat until dough is sticky. Spoon onto wax paper; wrap and refrigerate for several hours to overnight. Roll out dough ½-inch thick on a floured surface. Cut out shapes with floured cookie cutters; transfer to greased baking sheets. Bake at 350 degrees for 8 to 10 minutes, until edges are golden. Cool before frosting. Frost with Powdered Sugar Frosting, (below). Sprinkle with sugar. Add jellybeans for eyes and mouth. Makes 4 dozen.

Ghost-Like Treats

Frosted Pumpkin Drops

Butterscotch chips and pumpkin are the special ingredients in these delightful drop cookies!

1½ c. shortening
1 c. sugar
1 c. brown sugar, packed
2 eggs, beaten
1½ c. canned pumpkin
1 t. vanilla extract
3½ c. all-purpose flour
½ t. salt
1 t. baking soda
1 T. cinnamon
12-oz. pkg. butterscotch chips

In a large bowl, blend together shortening, sugars, eggs, pumpkin and vanilla. In a separate bowl, mix remaining ingredients except butterscotch chips. Gradually add flour mixture to shortening mixture, continuing to stir. Mix well; stir in butterscotch chips. Drop by tablespoonfuls onto ungreased baking sheets. Bake at 350 degrees for 11 to 13 minutes. Remove to wire racks. Frost with Powdered Sugar Frosting when cool. Let frosting dry completely before storing. Makes 3 to 4 dozen.

Powdered Sugar Frosting:

¼ c. butter, melted
2½ c. powdered sugar
1 t. vanilla extract
2 T. cream cheese, softened
1 to 2 T. milk

Mix all ingredients together until smooth, adding milk as needed.

Ooo. . . Oatmeal Wonders

Oatmeal and raisins combine to make these cookies ones they will ask for all year round!

¾ c. shortening
1 c. brown sugar, packed
½ c. sugar
2 eggs
¼ c. milk
2¼ c. all-purpose flour
1 t. baking soda
1 t. salt
1½ t. cinnamon
½ t. nutmeg
3 c. long-cooking oats, uncooked
1 c. raisins, chopped
Garnish: sugar

In a large bowl, beat together shortening and sugars until creamy. Add eggs, one at a time, beating after each addition. Add milk, beating until well blended and smooth; set aside. In a separate bowl, sift together flour, baking soda, salt and spices. Add flour mixture to shortening mixture; blend together. Fold in oats and raisins. Cover; refrigerate dough for one hour. Roll out to ¼-inch thickness on a lightly floured board. Cut with a floured 3-inch round cookie cutter. Place on greased baking sheets; sprinkle with sugar. Bake at 375 degrees for 10 to 12 minutes. Makes 3 dozen.

Ooo...
Oatmeal Wonders

All Hallow's Eve Feast

The rich colors of autumn and classic Halloween fare make this party a feast for the eyes as well as the body. Layer a trifle, create a cheesy pumpkin or form some bone-shaped bread. Have fun letting the spirits move you to prepare a spread for your family & friends that they just can't resist!

Getting Ready for the Party:

Setting up a buffet table with a variety of hot and cold foods takes planning. Make the cheese balls, candies and breads the day before. Have the sauces and veggies chopped and ready to go for the hot entrees and sides. That way you can stir up those last minute recipes the day of the party.

Party Activities:

Ask someone at the party who is a great story-teller to read a classic Halloween story or peom for the guests. Shut off the lights, gather around the fire and listen to the words of the piece, imagining what might be lurking outside.

The Invitation:

A simple candelabra cutout sets the stage for this eerie invitation. A full moon above announces the party. Instructions and patterns for making the invitation are on page 179.

Tablescapes:

Mimic the colors and textures of autumn with your linens and dishes. Choose linens that have texture such as woven fibers or burlap. Then add dishes in rich browns, soft greens and vivid oranges. Tuck in candles, gourds and mini pumpkins to complete the autumnal look.

"You wouldn't believe
On All Hallow Eve
What lots of fun we can make,
With apples to bob,
And nuts on the hob,
And a ring-and-thimble cake."

— CAROLYN WELLS

Rattlin' Rib Bones

Rattlin' Rib Bones

They will be coming back for more when you set out a platter of these tasty ribs!

2 c. zesty Italian salad dressing
$\frac{1}{4}$ c. soy sauce
1 T. garlic, minced
$\frac{1}{2}$ t. pepper
3 to 4 lbs. bone-in country-style pork ribs or chops
2 T. olive oil
2 to 3 onions, sliced into rings

In a small bowl, stir together salad dressing, soy sauce, garlic and pepper; set aside. In a skillet over medium heat, brown ribs in oil on both sides; drain. Arrange onion rings in an ungreased 13"x9" baking pan. Top with ribs; drizzle dressing mixture over top. Cover tightly with aluminum foil. Bake at 350 degrees for one hour, or until tender. Serves 6.

Easy Baked Corn

Yummy and easy! Garnish with a sprinkle of parsley or paprika.

2 c. frozen corn, thawed
2 eggs, beaten
$\frac{1}{4}$ c. butter, sliced
$\frac{3}{4}$ c. milk
3 T. sugar
2 T. all-purpose flour
$\frac{1}{4}$ t. salt

Place all ingredients in a blender or food processor; process to a slightly chunky consistency. Pour into a greased 2-quart casserole dish. Bake, uncovered, at 375 degrees for 45 minutes. Serves 6.

French Bread Femurs

Why settle for traditional French bread shapes when a femur bone shape can be so much more fun! The bones are easy to make and even easier to eat!

2 envs. active dry yeast
½ c. warm water, 110 to 115 degrees
2 c. hot water, 120 to 130 degrees
3 T. sugar
1 T. salt
⅓ c. oil
6 c. all-purpose flour, divided
1 egg white, beaten

In a cup, dissolve yeast in ½ cup warm water; set aside. In a large bowl, combine hot water, sugar, salt, oil and 3 cups flour; stir well. Stir in yeast mixture. Add remaining flour and stir well with a heavy spoon. Leave spoon in the dough; allow dough to rest 10 minutes. Stir; let dough rest another 10 minutes. Repeat this process 3 more times, making 5 times in all. Turn dough onto a lightly floured board. Knead just enough to coat dough with flour; divide dough into 5 equal balls. Roll out each ball into a 5-inch by 8-inch rectangle; roll up lengthwise, pinching together seams. Pinch and form ends to resemble the end of a bone. Place loaves seam-side down on 2 greased baking sheets, allowing room for both to rise. Cover; let rise in a warm place for 30 minutes, or until double in bulk. Brush with egg white. Bake at 400 degrees for about 30 minutes, or until crusty and golden. Remove to wire racks to cool. Makes 5 bone-shaped loaves.

French Bread Femurs

Sinfully Savory Chicken Casserole

The water chestnuts and almonds add crunch and the pimentos add a dash of color to this delicious casserole.

2 c. cooked chicken, diced
1½ c. long-cooking rice, cooked
10¾-oz. can cream of chicken soup
1 c. mayonnaise
8-oz. can water chestnuts, drained and chopped
2-oz. jar diced pimentos, drained
½ c. slivered almonds
2 t. onion, finely chopped
2 t. lemon juice
½ t. salt
½ t. pepper
1 c. bread cubes
3 T. butter, melted
garlic salt to taste

In a large bowl, mix together all ingredients except bread, butter and garlic salt. Spread mixture in a greased 13"x9" baking pan. Toss bread with butter; spread on a baking sheet. Bake at 400 degrees for 15 to 20 minutes, stirring after 10 minutes, until golden. Add garlic salt to taste; sprinkle over chicken mixture. Bake, uncovered, at 350 degrees for 30 to 40 minutes, until hot and bubbly. Serves 6 to 8.

TRICK OR TREAT!

Here's a Trick:
Purchase Halloween-shaped pasta to use in your mac & cheese. Pasta comes in all shapes during this fun season, and it will make your dish look extra festive!

Ghostly Potatoes

Cheese and potatoes combine to make a side that everyone will love!

¼ c. butter
¼ c. all-purpose flour
2 c. milk
8-oz. pkg. shredded sharp Cheddar cheese
1 t. salt
¼ t. pepper
5 potatoes, peeled and sliced
2 onions, sliced

Melt butter in a saucepan over low heat; blend in flour and cook for one minute. Whisk in milk. Cook, stirring constantly, until slightly thickened. Stir in cheese until melted. Add salt and pepper. Spread half of sauce in the bottom of a greased 13"x9" glass baking pan. Arrange potatoes and onions over sauce; top with remaining sauce. Bake, uncovered, at 350 degrees for about one hour, until potatoes are tender. Serves 8.

Monster Mac & Cheese

16-oz. pkg. medium shell macaroni, uncooked
16-oz. container sour cream
16-oz. container cottage cheese
1 bunch green onions, minced
1 egg, beaten
2 c. shredded Colby Jack cheese
2 c. shredded sharp Cheddar cheese
salt and pepper to taste
½ c. butter, melted and divided
1 c. Italian-flavored dry bread crumbs

Cook macaroni according to package directions; drain and set aside. Meanwhile, in a bowl, mix together sour cream, cottage cheese, onions and egg. Stir in cheeses, salt and pepper; add cooked macaroni and mix well. Coat a 13"x9" baking pan with 2 tablespoons melted butter. Spread mixture evenly in pan. Toss remaining butter with bread crumbs and sprinkle over top. Bake, uncovered, at 350 degrees for 30 to 40 minutes, until cheese is bubbly and bread crumbs are golden. Serves 10 to 12.

Harvest Pizza

Harvest Pizza

Everyone loves pizza! So make these mini pizzas and serve them to your Halloween guests!

3 c. bread flour
1 t. salt
½ t. sugar
1 c. warm water, 110 to 115 degrees
1 T. oil
1 T. quick-rising yeast
Garnish: favorite pizza toppings

In a bowl, combine flour, salt and sugar. Add water, oil and yeast to bowl. Knead by hand for 3 minutes; form into a ball. Cover and let rise until double in bulk, about an hour. Punch down dough; let rest for 4 minutes. Divide dough into 3 balls. On a floured surface, roll out each ball about ¼-inch thick. Place on an ungreased baking sheet. Let rise an additional 10 to 15 minutes. Spread Pizza Sauce over dough; add desired toppings. Place in a cold oven; turn to 500 degrees. Bake for 17 to 20 minutes, until golden. Serves 6.

Pizza Sauce:

8-oz. can tomato sauce
6-oz. can tomato paste
1¼ t. dried oregano
1¼ t. dried basil
1¼ t. garlic powder
1 t. salt

Stir together ingredients in a medium bowl.

Scarecrow Salad

This crunchy salad is fantastic! It adds color, flavor and texture to your Halloween buffet table.

1 head napa cabbage, sliced
6 green onions, chopped
½ c. butter or margarine
2 3-oz. pkgs. Oriental-flavored ramen
   noodles, crushed
½ c. sunflower kernels
¼ c. slivered almonds

Place cabbage and onions in a plastic zipping bag; refrigerate for one hour. In a saucepan over medium-low heat, melt butter or margarine and add crushed ramen noodles, contents of seasoning packets and remaining ingredients. Sauté until golden. Cool; drain on a paper towel. In a large bowl, combine cabbage mixture and noodle mixture. Pour Dressing over all; toss to coat. Serves 10 to 12.

Dressing:

1 c. oil
1 c. sugar
½ c. cider vinegar
2 T. soy sauce

Whisk ingredients together until well blended.

MAKE IT A PARTY!
Presenting the food is just as much fun as making it! When making your cheese ball pumpkin, set it on a pedestal plate and tuck fall leaves under the plate for an autumnal look.

Creepy Couscous

Little couscous pasta makes delightful dishes. This one is extra special because you can serve it hot or chilled.

10-oz. pkg. couscous, uncooked
¼ c. plus 1 T. olive oil, divided
½ c. lemon juice
1 t. Italian seasoning
15½-oz. can black beans, drained and rinsed
6-oz. pkg. baby spinach
1 t. salt
½ t. pepper

Prepare couscous according to package directions; drain and set aside. In a saucepan over medium heat, combine ¼ cup oil, lemon juice and Italian seasoning. Bring to a low boil; stir in beans and cook until warmed through. Meanwhile, add remaining oil to a skillet over medium heat; add spinach and cook until wilted. Add bean mixture to spinach and stir gently. Stir in couscous, salt and pepper. Serve immediately, or chill overnight and serve cold. Serves 8 to 10.

Hallowed Eve Cheese Pumpkin

2 8-oz. pkgs. shredded extra sharp Cheddar
   cheese
8-oz. pkg. cream cheese, softened
8-oz. container chive and onion cream cheese,
   softened
2 t. paprika
½ t. cayenne pepper
1 stalk broccoli, top removed
Garnish: finely chopped parsley, seeds such as
   poppy, sesame and fennel
assorted crackers

Combine all ingredients except broccoli and crackers. Shape mixture to resemble a pumpkin. Trim broccoli stalk, if needed, and press lightly into the top of the pumpkin for a stem. Use a knife to make vertical lines down the sides of the cheese ball. Press seeds into the sided of the pumpkin for texture. Serve with crackers. Serves 10 to 15.

Hallowed Eve Cheese Pumpkin

Harvest Pear Crisp

Pumpkin Gingerbread Trifle

Something different from that same old pumpkin pie! This luscious dessert will go quickly at your Halloween event!

14½-oz. pkg. gingerbread cake mix
3.4-oz. pkg. instant vanilla pudding mix
2 c. milk
15-oz. can pumpkin
½ t. cinnamon
16-oz. container frozen whipped topping, thawed and divided
3 1.4-oz. chocolate-covered toffee candy bars, crushed

Prepare and bake cake mix according to package directions. Cool; tear or cut cake into large chunks and set aside. Whisk together dry pudding mix and milk for 2 minutes, until thickened; gently stir in pumpkin and cinnamon. In a clear glass trifle bowl, layer half each of cake chunks, pudding mixture and whipped topping. Repeat layers, ending with topping. Garnish with crushed candy bars. Cover and refrigerate at least 3 hours before serving. Serves 12 to 16.

Harvest Pear Crisp

Select from the rich harvest of fall pears for this sweet dessert. Pears are softer and easier to peel and chop than apples and cook up soft and smooth.

3 c. Bartlett pears, peeled, cored and sliced
3 T. water
1 T. lemon juice
½ c. sugar, divided
½ c. plus 2 T. all-purpose flour, divided
1 t. cinnamon, divided
5 T. butter, chilled
¼ c. brown sugar, packed

In a bowl, combine pears, water, lemon juice, ¼ cup sugar, 2 tablespoons flour and ½ teaspoon cinnamon. Toss to mix. Spread in a lightly greased 8"x8" baking pan. In a separate bowl, cut together butter, brown sugar and remaining sugar, flour and cinnamon until crumbly. Sprinkle over pear mixture. Bake at 350 degrees for 45 minutes, or until pears are tender. Serves 6.

Pumpkin Gingerbread Trifle

Autumn Cake Balls

These pretty little treats will disappear fast!

18½-oz. pkg. red velvet cake mix
16-oz. container cream cheese frosting
16-oz. pkg. regular or white melting chocolate
food coloring

Prepare and bake cake mix according to package directions for a 13"x9" cake. Let cool. Crumble cooled cake into a large bowl. Stir in cream cheese frosting. Roll mixture into balls the size of quarters. Place on baking sheets and chill for several hours or overnight. Melt chocolate in double boiler. Dip cake balls into chocolate and place on waxed paper. Color chocolate with desired food coloring. Decorate tops with fall motifs by piping on top of cakes. Let stand until firm. Makes about 4 dozen.

Honey-Custard Bread Pudding

Everyone is sure to enjoy this old-fashioned bread pudding.

6 eggs, beaten
½ t. salt
4 c. milk
⅔ c. plus 2 T. honey, divided
2 T. butter, melted
Optional: ½ c. raisins
16-oz. loaf Vienna or
    French bread

Beat together eggs and salt in a small bowl; set aside. Bring milk just to a boil in a saucepan; let cool slightly. Stir ⅔ cup honey and butter into milk. Slowly stir eggs into milk mixture; add raisins, if using. Set aside. Tear bread into one-inch pieces and place in a greased 2½-quart casserole dish. Pour egg mixture over bread. Place casserole dish in another larger pan and pour hot water into the pan to come halfway up the side of the dish. Bake at 325 degrees for one hour, or until set. About 15 minutes before serving, drizzle remaining honey over top. Serves 8 to 10.

Spirited & Spiced Tea

6 c. water
¾ c. sugar
1 c. unsweetened instant
    tea mix
8 whole cloves
2 4-inch cinnamon sticks
2½ c. red fruit punch
¼ c. lemon juice

Combine water, sugar, instant tea mix, cloves and cinnamon sticks in a large saucepan. Bring to a boil over high heat, stirring occasionally. Boil for 2 to 4 minutes; remove whole spices, if desired. Stir in fruit punch and lemon juice; warm through. Serve hot. Serves 8.

Sinister Date Pudding

A dollop of whipped cream makes this rich and sweet dessert even sweeter!

2 c. all-purpose flour
2 c. sugar
2 c. dates, chopped
1 c. pecans, chopped
1 T. baking powder
1 c. milk
2 c. brown sugar, packed
2 T. butter, softened
1½ c. boiling water
Garnish: whipped cream, brown sugar

In a large bowl, mix together flour, sugar, dates, pecans, baking powder and milk; set aside. Combine brown sugar, butter and boiling water in a separate large bowl. Pour flour mixture over brown sugar mixture. Stir well and transfer to a greased deep 9"x9" baking pan. Bake at 350 degrees for 40 minutes. Top with whipped cream; sprinkle with brown sugar. Serves 12.

Sinister Date Pudding

The Great Pumpkin Dip

This sweet dip is perfect to serve with fall apple slices.

15-oz. can pumpkin
15-oz. jar creamy peanut butter
1½ c. brown sugar, packed
2 t. vanilla extract
⅛ t. cinnamon
⅛ t. nutmeg
apple slices

In a large bowl, mix all ingredients except apples until smooth. Cover and refrigerate at least 30 minutes before serving. Serve with apple slices. Serves 10.

"Sweet Potato" Candies

There's no actual sweet potato in these candies. Instead, they're shaped to look like little sweet potatoes.

1 c. butter
8 t. vanilla extract
2 t. salt
8 lbs. powdered sugar
20-oz. pkg. sweetened flaked coconut
1 c. milk, warmed
Garnish: cinnamon

Soften butter until almost melted. Mix together butter, vanilla and salt in a very large bowl. Stir in powdered sugar and coconut; mixture will be lumpy. Knead until smooth, adding milk a little at a time. Break off one-inch balls and roll into sweet potato shapes. Roll candies in cinnamon to coat. Place in a covered container; keep refrigerated. Makes about 14 to 15 dozen.

Countess of Chocolate Party

This party is all about chocolate! The celebration of this dark treat will soothe the soul indeed. From chocolate cookie desserts and dark chocolate kitty cakes to creamy fudge and devil's food cookies, you'll please all of the chocolate lovers at this Halloween party!

Getting Ready for the Party:
Candies and many cookies can be made days before the party and refrigerated or frozen until party time. That will leave you plenty of time to make the last minute desserts and drinks.

Party Activities:
Find a variety of chocolate types for your guests to taste test. Try milk chocolate, semi-sweet chocolate, white chocolate, unsweetened chocolate and more. Blindfold the players and see who can guess which is which!

The Invitation:
This invitation will be read and then consumed! Choose a flat chocolate bar and then design the invitation to fit. Tie a simple bow using brown or white tulle around the candy. This invitation is probably best hand-delivered, but it can be mailed in a sturdy envelope. For complete instructions for making the invitation see page 179.

Tablescapes:
Create a buffet table using all shades of browns and whites for the linens. Make the table covering a rich chocolate brown with bright white and orange dishes. Fill a white cake stand with all kinds of chocolate candies and use as the centerpiece.

"Money may talk, but chocolate sings."

— ANON

*"Forget love—
I'd rather fall in
chocolate!"*
— SANDRA J. DYKES

S'mores Brownies

Cemetery Cookie Dessert

Cemetery Cookie Dessert

Little cookies stand up to resemble little tombstones on this easy-to-make dessert.

18-oz. pkg. chocolate sandwich cookies, divided
8-oz. pkg. cream cheese, softened
3.4-oz. pkg. instant vanilla pudding mix
2 c. milk
1 c. powdered sugar
8-oz. container frozen whipped topping, thawed
Garnish: candy pumpkins

Set aside 6 to 7 cookies for garnish; crush remaining cookies. Spread ¼ of crushed cookies in the bottom of a lightly greased 13"x9" glass baking pan; set aside. In a large bowl, whip cream cheese with an electric mixer on medium speed. In a separate bowl, whisk together dry pudding mix and milk for 2 minutes, or until thickened; add to cream cheese along with powdered sugar and whipped topping. Beat until well blended. Spoon a layer of cream cheese mixture over cookies; add another layer of crushed cookies and another layer of cream cheese mixture. Repeat once more, for a total of 3 layers. Slice sides off reserved cookies and arrange on top. Add candy pumpkins. Cover and chill for 2 hours before serving. Keep refrigerated. Serves 10 to 12.

Halloween Kitty Cake

What a sweet kitty this is! The cake is baked, cut into shapes and then put together to make a purr-fect cake for any Halloween party.

2 c. sugar
½ c. shortening
2 eggs, beaten
2 c. all-purpose flour
1 t. salt
1 t. baking powder
1 T. baking soda
⅔ c. baking cocoa
2 c. boiling water
1 t. vanilla extract

In a large bowl, blend together sugar, shortening and eggs. Add flour, salt, baking powder and baking soda; beat well. Add cocoa, water and vanilla; pour into a greased 13"x9" baking pan. Bake at 350 degrees for 25 to 30 minutes, until cake tests done; cool. To make kitty-shaped cake, enlarge patterns, page 203, and cut out. Lay patterns on cake and cut around shapes. Place pieces on a large platter or cutting board and frost with Coconutty Pecan Frosting. Add pecan halves for eyes, ears and nose. Add coconut shreds for whiskers. Serves 8 to 10.

Coconutty Pecan Frosting:

1 c. evaporated milk
1 c. agave syrup or sugar
3 egg yolks
½ c. butter
1 t. vanilla extract
2 c. sweetened flaked coconut
1½ c. chopped pecans

In a saucepan over medium-low heat, combine all ingredients except coconut and pecans. Cook for about 12 minutes until thickened, stirring constantly. Remove from heat. Stir in coconut and pecans; beat until cool. Makes about 6 cups.

Halloween Kitty Cake

Chocolate-Almond Coffee

The combination of chocolate and coffee is almost too good to be true! Your guests will love it!

¼ c. baking cocoa
¼ c. instant coffee granules
½ c. sugar
¼ c. plus 2 T. finely ground almonds, divided
¼ t. salt
2 t. powdered non-dairy creamer
4½ c. milk
Garnish: whipped cream

In a blender, combine cocoa, instant coffee, sugar, ¼ cup ground almonds, salt and creamer. Cover and blend on high speed for 10 seconds. Heat milk in a 2-quart saucepan. Do not boil. Add cocoa mixture to hot milk; stir to combine. Pour into mugs. Top each serving with a dollop of whipped cream and a sprinkling of the remaining 2 tablespoons of the ground almonds. Serves 5 to 6.

Chocolate-Almond Coffee

Boo Goo Cake

This cake is a real treat…it is almost like eating a candy bar!

18½-oz. pkg. German chocolate cake mix
14-oz. can sweetened condensed milk
12¼-oz. jar caramel ice cream topping
2.1-oz. chocolate-covered crispy peanut butter candy bar, crushed and divided
8-oz. container frozen whipped topping, thawed
8-oz. pkg. cream cheese, softened
1 c. sugar

Prepare cake mix according to package directions; bake in a greased 13"x9" baking pan. While cake is baking, stir together condensed milk and caramel topping; set aside. Remove cake from oven. While cake is still hot, poke holes in top with a wooden spoon handle or skewer. Pour condensed milk mixture over cake; sprinkle with half of crushed candy bar. Refrigerate 2 to 3 hours. Mix together remaining ingredients until smooth; spread over chilled cake. Sprinkle with remaining candy bar. Keep refrigerated. Serves 16 to 20.

Dark Shadow Fudge

Every chocolate lover has a favorite fudge…and this one will be it! So velvety smooth and creamy, it is remarkably easy to make. Make plenty to give as treats when the kids come to the door!

4½ c. sugar
1½ c. butter or margarine
12-oz. can evaporated milk
3 6-oz. pkgs. semi-sweet chocolate chips
1 t. vanilla extract
13-oz. jar marshmallow creme
2 c. chopped pecans or walnuts
Halloween candies

In a large, heavy saucepan over medium-high heat, combine sugar, butter or margarine and evaporated milk. Bring to a rolling boil; boil for 5 minutes, stirring constantly. Remove from heat; add remaining ingredients. Stir until smooth and chocolate is melted except Halloween candies. Pour into a greased 15"x10" jelly-roll pan. Let stand overnight, or until firm. Cut into one-inch squares. Decorate with Halloween candies. Makes 5 pounds.

Dark Shadow Fudge

Ghost-Topped Fudge Pie

Rich and chocolaty, this pie is perfect for Halloween ghosts and goblins!

2 eggs
½ c. butter, melted and cooled slightly
¼ c. baking cocoa
¼ c. all-purpose flour
1 c. sugar
2 t. vanilla extract
⅓ c. semi-sweet chocolate chips
⅓ c. broken pecan pieces
9-inch pie crust
Garnish: whipped cream, mini chocolate chips

Beat eggs slightly; stir in melted butter. Add remaining ingredients except crust; pour into unbaked crust. Bake at 350 degrees for about 25 minutes, until firm. Cool before slicing. Top with whipped cream. Add mini chocolate chips for eyes to resemble ghost. Serves 8.

Fly-By-Night Cookies

Slice these cookies and bake them for a crowd!

2½ c. all-purpose flour
¼ t. baking soda
¾ c. butter, softened
1 c. sugar
1 egg, beaten
1 t. vanilla extract
1 T. milk
3 sqs. unsweetened baking chocolate, melted
½ c. chopped walnuts
½ c. chocolate chips

In a medium bowl, mix together flour and baking soda; set aside. In a large bowl, blend remaining ingredients, except chips, in order given. Add flour mixture to butter mixture; mix well. Form dough into a log about 2 inches in diameter and wrap in wax paper. Refrigerate overnight. Slice dough ⅛-inch thick; place on ungreased baking sheets. Bake at 400 degrees for 6 to 8 minutes. Cool. Melt chocolate chips and drizzle over cookies. Makes about 3 dozen.

Ghost-Topped Fudge Pie

Fly-By-Night Cookies

S'mores Brownies

S'mores Brownies

Make it feel like fall with this favorite combination of all-time-favorite ingredients.

18½-oz. pkg. brownie mix
3 c. mini marshmallows
4 whole graham crackers, coarsely broken
2 chocolate candy bars, broken into small
  pieces

Prepare brownies as directed on package; bake in a greased 13"x9" baking pan. As soon as brownies are removed from oven, sprinkle with marshmallows and graham cracker crumbs. Broil for 30 to 60 seconds, until marshmallows are golden. Watch carefully, as marshmallows will brown quickly. Sprinkle with candy bar pieces. Let cool for 15 minutes before cutting into squares. Serve warm. Makes 2 dozen.

Devil's Food Cookies

These quick-to-make cookies will make any dressed up devil (or angel) happy!

18½-oz. pkg. devil's food cake mix
½ c. oil
2 eggs, beaten
1 c. semi-sweet chocolate chips

Mix together dry cake mix and remaining ingredients. Drop by teaspoonfuls onto ungreased baking sheets. Bake at 350 degrees for 10 minutes, or until golden. Let cool on wire racks. Makes 3½ dozen.

Black Cauldron Cake

This cake is so good, it's magical!

18½-oz. pkg. German chocolate cake mix
3 eggs, beaten
1 c. water
⅓ c. oil
16-oz. can coconut-pecan frosting
Garnish: powdered sugar

Spray a Bundt® pan with non-stick vegetable spray; place on a baking sheet and set aside. In a bowl, combine dry cake mix, eggs, water and oil. Stir until well blended; beat with an electric mixer on medium speed for 2 minutes. Slowly beat in frosting until blended. Pour into prepared pan. Bake at 350 degrees for about 55 minutes, or until a toothpick inserted near center comes out clean. Allow cake to cool in pan for 5 minutes; invert onto a serving plate and allow to cool completely. Dust with powdered sugar before serving. Serves 10 to 12.

Cryptic Coffin Bars

These bars are so yummy…it's hard to eat just one!

¾ c. butter
2 c. brown sugar, packed
3 eggs, beaten
1 t. vanilla extract
2 c. self-rising flour
Optional: 1 c. chopped pecans, whipped
    topping

Place butter in a 13"x9" baking pan; set in a 350-degree oven to melt; let cool slightly. Place brown sugar in a bowl; pour melted butter over brown sugar. Add eggs, vanilla, flour and nuts, if using; mix well and pour back into same baking pan. Bake at 350 degrees for 10 minutes. Reduce oven temperature to 325 degrees; bake for an additional 25 to 30 minutes. Cool completely; slice into bars. Top with whipped topping, if desired. Makes 1½ to 2 dozen.

Mocha Coffee Mix

This simple, old-fashioned recipe warms the heart and soul on a cool Halloween night.

2 c. powdered non-dairy creamer
1½ c. hot chocolate mix
1½ c. instant coffee granules
1 t. cinnamon
½ t. nutmeg

Sift together creamer, hot chocolate mix, instant coffee, cinnamon and nutmeg; store in airtight container. To use: stir one tablespoon of mixture into one cup of hot water; adjust to taste. Makes about 5 cups.

> MAKE IT A PARTY!
> Because this party is all about chocolate, find sayings about chocolate and print them for guests to read aloud as they sample the wonderful goodies you are sharing!

Chapter 4

Wickedly Wonderful Treats

(Ghoulish Goodies to Concoct)

Whether they are coming to the door for a treat or for a celebration, greet them with a goodie you make yourself. Roll some sticky caramel apples, slice some spiderweb cookies, fry some doughnut holes, dip some cookie pops or stir up a pizza dip. No matter what treats you choose to make, you'll enjoy creating these Halloween recipes as much as they enjoy devouring them. Get everyone involved in the spirit of preparing for Halloween fun. There's no trick to it!

"Bring forth the raisins and the nuts,
Tonight All Hallows' Spectre struts
Along the moonlit way."

— JOHN KENDRICK BANGS

Sinking Doughnuts
& Doughnut Howls

Sinking Doughnuts & Doughnut Howls

These easy-to-make doughnuts become super Halloweeny when dipped in orange and white frosting.

2 12-oz. tubes refrigerated biscuits
oil for frying
2 c. powdered sugar
2 to 3 T. water
orange food coloring
chocolate candy coating

Using a thimble, remove the center of each biscuit; set aside. Pour ½ inch of oil into a deep skillet over medium-high heat. Fry biscuits and holes in hot oil until lightly golden, about 30 seconds. Turn and cook on second side; drain on paper towels. Let cool completely. Combine powdered sugar and enough water to make a glaze; divide between 2 bowls and tint with different food coloring. Dip doughnuts in glaze. Melt the candy coating and drizzle over the frosting. Makes 20.

Lookie-Lookie
Cookie Pops

½ c. butter, softened
½ c. shortening
1 c. sugar
1 c. powdered sugar
2 eggs, beaten
¾ c. oil
2 t. vanilla extract
4 c. all-purpose flour
1 t. baking soda
1 t. salt
1 t. cream of tartar
candy coating: white, orange and dark
   chocolate
small candies, lollipop sticks

Beat butter and shortening until fluffy; add sugars, beating well. Beat in eggs, oil and vanilla. In a separate bowl, combine flour and remaining ingredients except candy coating, candies and sticks. Cover and chill 2 hours. Shape dough into 1½ inch balls. Place 2 inches apart on ungreased baking sheets. Insert a stick about one inch into each ball. Bake at 350 degrees for 10 to 11 minutes, until set. Let cool 2 minutes on baking sheets; cool completely on wire racks. Coat with melted candy coating. Decorate with candies. Pipe whiskers with white candy coating. Makes 4½ dozen.

HALLOWEEN TIP
Here's a quick way to candy coat your cookie pops: Place a cooling rack up high supported between 2 cake mix boxes. Cover with waxed paper. After dipping the cookie pops, poke the stick through the waxed paper on the rack and let cool.

Lookie-Lookie
Cookie Pops

Skullduggery
Squares

Skullduggery Squares

*The real pumpkin in these little bars makes them
moist and full of color!*

12-oz. can evaporated milk
3 eggs, beaten
2 t. pumpkin pie spice
½ t. salt
1 c. sugar
15-oz. can pumpkin
18½-oz. pkg. yellow cake mix
½ c. butter, sliced
**Garnish: whipped topping, candy sprinkles,
  colored sugar**

Combine all ingredients except cake mix, butter
and garnish. Pour into a greased 13"x9" pan.
Sprinkle on dry cake mix; do not stir. Dot with
butter. Bake at 350 degrees for 30 to 35 minutes.
Serve with whipped topping. Decorate with
candy sprinkles or colored sugar. Makes 20
squares.

Sticky-Sweet Caramel Apples

Use small apples to make caramel apples for sweet party favors! You'll be able to make 10 to 12 mini apples with this recipe.

4 to 6 wooden treat sticks
4 to 6 Gala or Jonagold apples
14-oz. pkg. caramels, unwrapped
2 T. milk
Optional: candy sprinkles, chopped nuts,
    candy corn, mini candy-coated chocolates

Insert sticks into apples; set aside. Combine caramels and milk in a microwave-safe bowl. Microwave on high setting, uncovered, for 2 minutes, stirring once. Allow to cool briefly. Roll each apple quickly in caramel, turning to coat. Set apples to dry on lightly greased wax paper. When partially set, roll in toppings, if desired. Makes 4 to 6.

Sticky-Sweet
Caramel Apples

Serpent's Pizza
Snacks

Serpent's Pizza Snacks

Who needs frozen pizza rolls when it's a snap to make this yummy homemade version? Add any little toppings you like. Your Halloween friends will love them!

8-oz. tube refrigerated crescent rolls
⅓ c. pizza sauce
¼ c. grated Parmesan cheese
16 slices pepperoni, divided
⅓ c. shredded mozzarella cheese, divided

Unroll rolls but do not separate; press perforations to seal. Spread pizza sauce evenly over rolls, leaving a one-inch border. Sprinkle with Parmesan cheese. Roll up dough jelly-roll fashion, starting with the short side. Using a sharp knife, cut into 15 slices. Place slices cut-side down on a greased baking sheet. Top each piece with one pepperoni slice and one teaspoon mozzarella cheese. Bake at 375 degrees for 9 to 11 minutes, until edges are golden and cheese is melted. Serves 16.

HALLOWEEN TIP

Make these pizza snacks veggie-style by adding chopped green pepper or chopped spinach to each piece instead of the pepperoni. Yum!

Pumpkin Patch Cookies

The frosting on these cookies makes them super sweet and super yummy!

1 c. shortening
1 c. sugar
1 c. canned pumpkin
1 egg, beaten
2 t. vanilla extract, divided
2 c. all-purpose flour
½ t. salt
1 t. baking soda
1 t. baking powder
1 t. cinnamon
8-oz. pkg. cream cheese, softened
¼ c. butter, softened
2 c. powdered sugar
Garnish: orange sugar

Blend together shortening, sugar, pumpkin and egg; stir in one teaspoon vanilla. Combine remaining ingredients except cream cheese, butter and powdered sugar. Gradually beat flour mixture into pumpkin mixture. Drop by rounded tablespoonfuls onto greased baking sheets. Bake at 350 degrees for 12 to 15 minutes; cool completely. Blend together cream cheese and butter; stir in remaining vanilla. Gradually add powdered sugar until fluffy. Spread cookies with frosting. Sprinkle with orange sugar. Makes 2 to 3 dozen.

Pumpkin Patch Cookies

Spiderweb Cookies

Spiderweb Cookies

These cookies are simply delicious all by themselves. But add some frosting and a black frosting spiderweb and you have a party cookie!

½ c. butter or margarine
1 c. sugar
2 t. vanilla extract
1 egg, beaten
1¾ c. all-purpose flour
½ t. baking soda
½ t. salt
½ c. chopped pecans or English walnuts
2 c. powdered sugar
2 to 3 T. water
black decorator tube frosting
toothpick

Beat together butter or margarine and sugar until mixture is fluffy. Add vanilla and egg, blending well. Whisk together flour, baking soda and salt; stir in nuts. Gradually add to butter mixture; beat well. Place dough on wax paper; shape into 2 long rolls, 2 inches in diameter. Chill overnight, or, if desired, wrap and freeze for future use. Slice dough ¼-inch thick; bake on ungreased baking sheets at 400 degrees for about 7 minutes, or until lightly golden. Cool. Combine powdered sugar and enough water to make a thin frosting. Frost cookies. (See Photo A.) Before frosting has set, make circles using the black decorator tube frosting. Add a dot in the center if desired. (See Photo B.) Use the toothpick to pull the black frosting from the center to the edges making the frosting look like spiderwebs. (See Photo C.) Let frosting dry before stacking. Makes 6 dozen.

A

B

C

HALLOWEEN TIP
Who says cobwebs always have to be black? Gel frosting comes in a variety of colors. So make your webs to match your Halloween color theme.

see page 157.

HALLOWEEN TIP

To be sure you are ready for Halloween, make some of your treats ahead of time and freeze until the big day. Most cookies freeze well as do some cakes. Just store them in single layers in freezer containers. Most baked items will keep for up to one month and retain good flavor. Baking ahead of time will leave you time to make some fun Halloween treat bags to give to those special Halloween trick and treaters. For some fun ideas for treat bags, see page 157.

Spicy Pumpkin Warm-Up

Try serving this sweet drink either hot or cold in glasses or cups rimmed with graham cracker crumbs for a fun party drink!

2 pts. whipping cream
½ c. sugar
⅓ c. canned pumpkin
1 t. pumpkin pie spice
½ t. vanilla extract
Garnish: whipped cream, additional pumpkin pie spice

Combine cream and sugar in a saucepan over medium heat; stir until sugar is dissolved. Whisk in pumpkin until well blended; add pumpkin pie spice and vanilla. Simmer for 10 to 15 minutes, until mixture is warm. Pour into mugs. Serve with a dollop of whipped cream and a sprinkle of spice. Serves 4 to 6.

Spicy Pumpkin
Warm-Up

Decadent Cookie Dough Brownies

Chocolate lovers will adore these yummy brownies…they are simply amazing!

2 c. sugar
½ c. baking cocoa
1 c. oil
2 t. vanilla extract
1½ c. all-purpose flour
½ t. salt
4 eggs, beaten
Optional: ½ c. chopped walnuts
1 c. semi-sweet chocolate chips
1 T. shortening
Garnish: ¼ c. chopped walnuts

Mix all ingredients together except chocolate chips, shortening and garnish. Pour into a greased 13"x9" baking pan and bake at 350 degrees for 30 minutes. Cool completely.

Prepare Cookie Dough and spread over cooled brownies. Add chocolate chips to a microwave-safe bowl and melt on low. Add shortening, stirring to blend. Drizzle over brownies. Garnish with nuts. Refrigerate until glaze is firm. Serves 8 to 12.

Cookie Dough:

½ c. butter, softened
¼ c. sugar
1 t. vanilla extract
½ c. brown sugar, packed
2 T. milk
1 c. all-purpose flour
¼ c. mini chocolate chips

Mix together all ingredients in a small bowl.

Chocolate Witch Cauldrons

Top these adorable "cauldrons" with gummy worms for a real treat!

24 chocolate sandwich cookies, crushed
½ c. butter, melted
1 c. milk
¾ c. whipping cream
3.3-oz. pkg. instant white chocolate pudding mix
10 drops green food coloring
½ c. semi-sweet mini chocolate chips
12 pretzel sticks

Place foil baking cups in each of 12 muffin cups; set aside. Combine cookie crumbs and melted butter in a bowl; stir to mix. Spoon 2 heaping tablespoonfuls into each baking cup; press into the bottom and up the sides. Beat together milk, whipping cream, pudding mix and food coloring with an electric mixer on high speed for one minute; stir in chocolate chips. Spoon pudding mixture into prepared muffin cups. Chill one hour. Before serving, place a pretzel stick into each "cauldron." Makes 12.

Black Kitty Cat Cupcakes

Don't be afraid of these black cats. . .they are devilishly good!

18½-oz. pkg. devil's food cake mix
12 chocolate sandwich cookies, quartered
16-oz. can dark chocolate frosting
48 yellow or green jellybeans
24 black jellybeans
24 pieces black rope licorice

Prepare and bake cake according to package directions for cupcakes using paper liners. Cool for 10 minutes, then remove and place on wire racks to cool completely. Frost tops of cupcakes; insert 2 cookie pieces for ears and lightly frost each. Arrange yellow or green jellybeans for eyes and a black jellybean for the nose. Cut each piece of black licorice into thirds, then in half. Place 3 halves on each side of the nose for whiskers. Makes 2 dozen.

Black Kitty Cat
Cupcakes

Bloodcurdling Pizza Dip

Don't let the name worry you, this savory dip is the best! Serve it with toasted baguettes, or pita bread.

8-oz. pkg. cream cheese, softened
1 t. Italian seasoning
1 c. shredded mozzarella cheese
¾ c. grated Parmesan cheese
8-oz. can pizza sauce
¼ c. red or green pepper, diced
Optional: cooked sausage or chopped
   pepperoni
assorted crackers

Blend together cream cheese and seasoning; spread on the bottom of an ungreased 9"x9" baking pan. Combine cheeses and sprinkle half over cream cheese mixture. Spoon on pizza sauce, spreading to edges. Sprinkle with pepper and, if desired, sausage or pepperoni slices. Top with remaining cheese mixture. Bake at 350 degrees for 15 to 20 minutes. Serve with crackers. Serves 10 to 12.

Bloodcurdling
Pizza Dip

Cunning Citrus Cake

Cunning Citrus Cake

This autumn recipe comes together in no time and never fails to impress. If you are a real citrus lover, try adding one tablespoon orange zest and 2 tablespoons of freshly squeezed lemon juice to the pudding mixes.

18½-oz. pkg. yellow cake mix
2 c. milk
1¼ c. water
2 3.4-oz. pkgs. instant lemon pudding mix
⅓ c. sugar
Garnish: 2 T. powdered sugar

Prepare cake batter as directed on package; pour into a greased 13"x9" baking pan. Set aside. Pour milk and water into a large bowl; stir in dry pudding mixes and sugar. Beat with a wire whisk for 2 minutes, or until well blended. Pour milk mixture into baking pan over cake batter; do not stir. Place baking pan on a baking sheet to catch any bubble-overs. Bake at 350 degrees for 55 minutes to one hour, until a toothpick inserted near the center comes out clean. Cool for 20 minutes to allow sauce to thicken. Dust with powdered sugar. Store leftovers in the refrigerator. Serves 16.

Note: To make a Halloween shape on the top of the cake, cut a simple pattern from parchment paper. Lay the pattern on top of the cake and dust with powdered sugar. Remove the paper pattern.

Wizard Hats

Wizard Hats

Make this treat for the kids to take to school for a fun Halloween treat!

3 c. puffed rice cereal
1-oz. sq. unsweetened baking chocolate
1 c. mini marshmallows
3 T. corn syrup
8 flat cookies such as cookies on page 136 before frosting
12-oz. pkg. semi-sweet chocolate chips
Garnish: candy sprinkles, licorice, candy

Pour cereal into a shallow pan; bake at 350 degrees for 10 minutes. Transfer to a bowl lightly coated with non-stick vegetable spray; set aside. Meanwhile, in a saucepan over low heat, combine chocolate and marshmallows; cook and stir until melted. Add corn syrup; stir well. Pour chocolate mixture over cereal; stir to coat cereal evenly. Divide mixture into 8 portions; shape each into a cone. Add chocolate chips to the top of a double boiler over boiling water; melt chocolate, stirring occasionally. Dip cones into melted chocolate, turning to coat. Place on cookie. Brush cookie with melted chocolate. Garnish with sprinkles, licorice and candy; cool. Makes 8.

Wicked Chocolate Wedges

This rich and chocolaty pie is topped off with a dollop of whipped cream and candy corn. But a sprinkle of chocolate curls makes it decadent!

⅔ c. milk
¾ c. semi-sweet chocolate chips
2 T. cornstarch
¼ c. cold water
14-oz. can sweetened condensed milk
3 eggs, beaten
1 t. vanilla extract
3 T. butter
8-inch chocolate cookie crust
Garnish: frozen whipped topping, candies

Pour milk into a 3-quart saucepan over medium heat. Heat just until milk begins to bubble around the edges. Do not boil. Remove from heat and whisk in chocolate chips until melted. Cool slightly. Stir cornstarch into cold water until dissolved. Whisk cornstarch mixture, sweetened condensed milk, eggs and vanilla into chocolate mixture. Bring to a boil over medium heat, whisking constantly. Boil one minute or until mixture thickens and is smooth; do not overcook. Remove from heat and whisk in butter. Spoon mixture into pie crust. Cover and chill 8 hours. Top with whipped topping and candies. Serves 8.

Wicked Chocolate Wedges

Chapter 5

Devilish Disguises

(Costumes & Treat Bags for Fun & Fright)

Go scavenging in the fabric box for some freaky, fun fabrics to conjure up costumes and treat bags this year. Whether you are concocting designs for your sweet little monsters or for the big, bad grown-ups, make it easy by starting with some purchased basics. Purchased sweatshirts, hoodies, leotards, onesies and headbands can make it easy to get the look you want without hours of sewing…leaving you time for some tricks and treats of your own.

"Clothes make a statement. Costumes tell a story."

Costumes for the Little Ghouls & Boys

CREATING CAPTIVATING COSTUMES for the little ones is no trick when you start with sweatshirts, hoodies, hats, leotards and onesies…and then use easy-to-work-with fabrics like felt and tulle for embellishments. So let the fun begin and get ready to trick or treat!

NIGHT-OWL COSTUME

Dressing up as an owl is a hoot! He'll be saying, "Whoo, whoooooo" with big smiles when he wears his colorful owl costume made from a purchased hat and sweatshirt and a rainbow of colorful felt.

The little fleece hat is embellished with big owl eyes made from layers of felt with a little orange beak added in the front.

The costume can easily be adjusted for any size sweatshirt. Just extend the feathered strips to stretch across the chest and elongate the wings to span the sweatshirt sleeves. Instructions start on page 179. Patterns start on page 199.

"*The witches fly* Across the sky, The *owls* go, Who? Who? Who? The black cats yowl, And green ghosts howl, Scary *Halloween* to you!"

— NINA WILLIS WALTER

"A grandmother pretends she doesn't know who you are on Halloween."

— ERMA BOMBECK

LITTLE MISS MERMAID

Let the little ones get in on the fun with a quick and comfortable costume they'll love to wear. The clam shell bikini top is appliquéd onto a long-sleeve onesie and the printed skirt offers plenty of room for baby kicks. The fin is made from blue felt with an appliquéd trim. A purchased hat decorated with a simple felt starfish finishes the sweet costume. Instruction are on page 180 and patterns are on page 198.

A LITTLE SQUIRRELLY

A gray hoodie, mittens and sweatpants make this little squirrel easy to pull together in no time! A big fluffy tail and ears and paws made from fun fur is the trick to making this cozy little guy soft and sweet. Fun fur also trims the hood, and little felt circles on the inside of the mittens make paws that grasp goodies even easier! Instructions are on page 181 and patterns start on page 202.

JUST-FOR-ME PRINCESS COSTUMES

You'll be her fairy godmother when you make her a princess dress that is all about her! Whether she loves strawberries, candy corn or pretty butterflies, you can make her costume with just a little tulle and some brightly colored trims.

Making a magical tutu is easier than you think! Strips of brightly colored or white tulle are simply looped onto an elastic band. Then the ribbons, tiny pom-poms and butterflies are sewn or glued to the finished skirt. Headbands are adorned with painted clay embellishments or pretty purchased butterflies. Little beaded necklaces add that special sparkle that every little girl loves!

A magic wand finishes the perfect-little-princess look. Instructions start on page 182 and patterns are on page 194.

"Life itself is the most wonderful fairy tale of all."

— HANS CHRISTIAN ANDERSEN

Delightfully Frightening Headbands & Masks

DON'T HAVE TIME for a complete costume get-up this year? Try making a quick head topper or color a silly mask. Headbands can become your best friend when you add some spooky decorations. Choose embellishments that give you that nightmare look you have always dreamed about!

WITCH HAT HEADBAND
This sweet little witch hat won't weigh you down! The little hat is made from a square of sparkling black felt and multi-colored feathers are tucked underneath.

BONES AND ROSES TOPPER
Form lightweight clay into bones and combine with roses for a bona fide beautiful costume topper.

BIRD ON A BRANCH HEADBAND
You are sure to get second glances all night long with a black bird perched on your head. This easy topper is sure to become your friend!

SPIDER VEIL
Here's a chance to be a bride again and sport some little creepy crawlers at the same time. Luckily these little spiders are of the plastic species.

MUMMY BRIDE HEADBAND
Mummy bandages flow down with strings of pearls as dead roses top this sinister headband.

Instructions for all of the headbands start on page 183.

ANIMAL FRIENDS

Whether you want to oink, peep or meow, you'll love to color and wear these wonderfully silly paper masks. Color the masks with marker, colored pencil or crayon in the colors that you choose to personalize your little animal friend. Then add a little 3-D embellishment to make the masks even merrier. The Pink Pig has a little piece of raffia glued by the nose for straw. The Baby Chick has a feather glued to the top of her head, and the Curious Kitty has a tell-tale feather attached by her mouth. The masks are punched on the side and then tied on with a piece of string. For all of the patterns see page 196.

Terrorific Treat Bags

GOODIE GETTING is lots more fun when you have a special treat bag! Whether you want to tote along a special little bag to capture those goodies at the door, or you want to just carry the tote for some Halloween style, you'll have fun constructing these clever little goodie holders for those very special trick-or-treaters.

BLACK KITTY TREAT BAG AND HAPPY SKELETON TOTE

A few embroidery stitches turn plain black or white felt into darling goodie bags for Halloween fun. Inspired by vintage Halloween decorations, wool felt is easy to sew and ideal for embroidery. The double thickness makes a sturdy bag that can handle a busy night of trick and treating. Instructions start on page 185 and patterns are on page 197.

Chapter 6

Fiendish Finger Foods
(Just Little Bites!)

Little fingers and big fingers alike will love to grab these Halloween morsels and eat them up! Whether you want to fill a bowl with cool goodies like snack mixes, pumpkin seeds and caramel corn, or keep a plate hot with chicken fingers, bacon wraps and egg rolls, you'll please them all with these little quick-to-gobble-up treats.

"Pixie, kobold, elf and sprite, All are on their rounds tonight; In the wan moon's silver ray, Thrives their helter-skelter play."

— JOEL BENTON

Autumn Caramel Corn

Autumn Caramel Corn

So rich and sweet...you can't get enough of this little finger food!

1 c. brown sugar, packed
1/4 c. dark corn syrup
1/2 c. butter
1/2 t. salt
1/2 t. vanilla extract
1/4 t. baking soda
3 qts. popped popcorn

Combine brown sugar, corn syrup, butter and salt in a saucepan. Bring to a boil over medium-high heat, cook for 5 minutes. Stir in vanilla and baking soda. Place popcorn in a very large bowl; pour brown sugar mixture over popcorn and toss to coat. Spoon into a buttered 15"x10" jelly-roll pan. Bake at 250 degrees for one hour, stirring every 15 minutes. Makes 3 quarts.

Vanishing Pretzels

These little finger foods will cast a spell on everyone who devours them!

12-oz. bag mini pretzel twists
¼ c. butter
¼ t. garlic powder
¼ c. grated Parmesan cheese

Place pretzels in a large microwave-safe bowl; set aside. Combine butter and garlic powder in a one-cup glass measuring cup. Microwave on high setting 30 to 45 seconds; stir to combine. Drizzle mixture over pretzels and lightly toss. Sprinkle with cheese; toss again. Microwave on high setting 3 to 4 minutes, stirring once or twice. Cool; store in a tightly covered container. Serves 12.

HALLOWEEN TIP

Choose whatever kind of cheese you like to add to this easy snack. Simply shred the cheese, toss and microwave. There will be no problem with this little treat disappearing.

Vanishing Pretzels

Spooky-Sweet Candy Corn

Making this candy corn is almost like magic. You won't believe how easy it is, and your trick-or-treaters will be impressed!

1 c. sugar
⅓ c. butter
⅔ c. light corn syrup
1 t. vanilla extract
2½ c. powdered sugar
¼ t. salt
⅓ c. powdered milk
red and yellow food coloring

Combine sugar, butter and corn syrup in a heavy saucepan over medium heat. Bring to a boil, stirring constantly. Reduce heat to low and boil 5 minutes, stirring occasionally. Remove from heat and add vanilla; set aside. Combine powdered sugar, salt and powdered milk; stir into sugar mixture. Let stand about 20 minutes, or until cool enough to handle. Divide dough into 3 equal parts and place in bowls. Wearing plastic gloves, knead desired amount of yellow food coloring into one bowl of dough; knead desired amount of yellow and red into the second bowl to create orange. Leave remaining bowl uncolored. Roll each portion of dough into a long, thin rope of equal lengths. Arrange dough ropes side-by-side; press seams together using a rolling pin. Cut into triangles with a sharp knife; shape edges to resemble corn kernels. Set aside until firm; store in an airtight container. Makes about one pound.

Spooky-Sweet Candy Corn

Eat-It-Up Snack Mix

Eat-It-Up Snack Mix

Family, friends and coworkers will love "goblin" up this yummy snack mix! Make it for Halloween parties and fall gatherings.

4 c. bite-size crispy cereal squares
4 c. popped kettle corn or regular popcorn
1 c. honey-roasted peanuts
1 c. salted roasted pumpkin seeds
¼ c. butter
6 T. brown sugar, packed
2 T. light corn syrup
¼ t. vanilla extract
¼ t. pumpkin pie spice
1 c. candy corn and/or candy pumpkins

In a 4-quart microwave-safe bowl, mix together cereal, popcorn, peanuts and pumpkin seeds; set aside. In a microwave-safe bowl, combine butter, brown sugar, corn syrup and vanilla. Microwave, uncovered, on high setting for about 2 minutes, until mixture is boiling; stir after one minute. Stir in spice. Pour over cereal mixture and stir until evenly coated. Microwave 5 minutes, stirring after every minute. Spread on wax paper. Let cool for about 15 minutes, stirring occasionally to break up any large pieces. Add candy and toss to mix. Store in an airtight container. Makes about 11 cups.

Zombie Fingers

Zombie Fingers

Orange nails are so pretty on fingers…and these are nutritious as well!

7 saltine crackers
2 T. grated Parmesan cheese
⅛ t. garlic powder
8 chicken tenders
½ c. Italian salad dressing
sliced carrots

Place crackers, cheese and garlic in a blender or food processor; blend until crumbly. Dip chicken in Italian dressing; roll in cracker mixture. Arrange on a lightly greased baking sheet and bake at 350 degrees for 20 minutes. Just before serving add a sliced carrot to the end of the chicken to resemble a fingernail. Serves 3 to 4.

Coffee Toffee

1 c. espresso beans, slightly crushed
½ c. butter
¾ c. brown sugar, packed
1 c. semi-sweet chocolate chips

Sprinkle crushed coffee beans evenly over the bottom of an ungreased 8"x8" baking pan. Combine butter and brown sugar in a saucepan over medium-low heat; bring to a boil. Cook, stirring constantly, for exactly 7 minutes. Immediately pour mixture over crushed beans and quickly spread from side to side. Sprinkle evenly with chocolate chips. Cover pan and let sit for 5 minutes. Remove cover and spread melted chocolate chips evenly over toffee. Refrigerate for one to 3 hours. Invert pan and break toffee into pieces. Makes about one pound.

Mummy Munch

Every party goer will love to grab a handful of this munchy goodie!

9 c. favorite cereal or small crackers
4 c. popped popcorn
1½ c. dry roasted peanuts
1 c. brown sugar, packed
½ c. butter
½ c. light corn syrup
1 t. vanilla extract
½ t. baking soda
2 c. candy-coated chocolates

Lightly grease a large roasting pan; stir in cereal or crackers, popcorn and peanuts. In a saucepan over medium heat, mix together brown sugar, butter and corn syrup. Bring to a boil and cook, without stirring, for 5 minutes. Remove from heat; add vanilla and baking soda. Mix well and pour over mixture in roasting pan; toss to coat. Bake at 250 degrees for 45 minutes, stirring every 15 minutes. Cool completely; add candy, tossing to mix. Store in an airtight container. Serves 12 to 16.

To make the container:

Tear pieces of white paper into strips and glue around a clear plastic cup, leaving some of the cup showing. Glue on googly eyes. Let dry.

Mummy Munch

Snackin' Pumpkin Seeds

Every Halloween carved pumpkins appear. Now you know what to do with the seeds!

2 c. pumpkin seeds
3 T. butter, melted
1¼ t. salt
½ t. Worcestershire sauce

In an ungreased shallow baking pan, combine all ingredients; stir to mix. Bake at 250 degrees for about 2 hours, stirring occasionally, until seeds are crisp, dry and golden. Cool completely; store in an airtight container. Makes 2 cups.

Gooey Gummy Worms

Snackin' Pumpkin Seeds

Gooey Gummy Worms

This is such a fun recipe to do with kids…and you'll love to serve them and hear the giggles. If you're a real candy connoisseur, you might like to make these in candy molds for fancier gummy candy.

1 c. boiling water
2 .3-oz. pkgs. favorite-flavor sugar-free gelatin mix
2 .3-oz. pkgs. favorite-flavor unsweetened drink mix
3 1-oz. envs. unflavored gelatin

Coat an 8"x8" baking pan with non-stick vegetable spray; set aside. In a bowl, combine all ingredients and stir until dissolved. Pour into prepared pan. Cover and refrigerate for 2 to 3 hours, until completely set. Cut into ¼-inch wide strips to form thin "worms" for serving as is or decorating other treats. Makes about 2½ dozen.

Ghostly Macaroons

So easy to make, your guests will love these chewy little ghost-like morsels of coconut.

4 egg whites, beaten
1 t. vanilla extract
⅛ t. almond extract
¾ c. sugar
¼ t. salt
3 c. sweetened flaked coconut

In a large bowl, whisk together all ingredients except coconut. Add coconut; mix well. Drop by rounded teaspoonfuls onto parchment paper-lined baking sheets. Bake at 325 degrees for about 25 minutes, or until set and golden; rotate baking sheets between upper and lower oven racks halfway through baking time. Cool on baking sheets for one minute; transfer to wire racks and cool completely. Store in an airtight container. Makes about 3½ dozen.

Ghostly Macaroons

Rye Tombstones

Make these tasty little appetizers for parties. They are a truly to-die-for treat!

1 lb. ground beef
1 lb. mild ground pork sausage
1 lb. pasteurized process cheese spread, cubed
1 t. dried oregano
½ t. garlic salt
½ t. Worcestershire sauce
1 loaf sliced party rye bread
green pepper strips
sliced olives

Brown beef and sausage in a skillet over medium heat; drain. Add remaining ingredients except bread; mix well and stir until cheese is melted. Arrange bread slices on ungreased baking sheets. Spread with beef mixture. Top with pepper strips and olives to spell R-I-P. Bake at 350 degrees for 20 minutes. Rounds may be reheated in the oven as needed; cover with aluminum foil before reheating. Makes 2½ dozen.

Graveyard Crunch

Halloween celebrations are just a little bit sweeter with this tasty treat!

¼ c. pancake syrup
2 T. butter, softened
¼ t. cinnamon
4 c. cocoa-flavored crispy rice cereal
1 c. dry-roasted peanuts
2 c. mini marshmallows
1 c. candy corn
1 c. candy-coated chocolates

Mix together syrup, butter and cinnamon in a large microwave-safe bowl. Microwave, uncovered, on high setting for one minute; stir until butter is completely melted. Add cereal and peanuts; toss to mix. Spread on a lightly greased 15"x10" jelly-roll pan. Bake at 300 degrees for 30 minutes, stirring after 15 minutes. Cool completely. Break into pieces; toss with remaining ingredients. Store in an airtight container. Makes 9 cups.

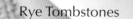
Rye Tombstones

HALLOWEEN TIP
Present these little rye treats on a tarnished silver tray for some Halloween fun. What a good excuse not to polish the tray for a party!

Marinated Eyeballs

Marinated Eyeballs

A few simple ingredients can do wonders for ordinary olives. . .you'll be amazed at the flavor!

2 c. green olives, drained
1 to 2 cloves garlic, slivered
3 thin slices lemon
1 t. whole peppercorns
3 bay leaves
¼ c. wine vinegar
¼ to ½ c. olive oil

In a wide-mouthed jar with a lid, combine all ingredients except oil. Add enough oil to cover ingredients. Secure lid. Refrigerate at least 24 hours to blend flavors before serving. Makes 2 cups.

Knuckle Tips

These little goodies will disappear in no time! The brown sugar adds just the perfect amount of sweetness to these tasty little treats!

1 lb. bacon
14-oz. pkg. mini smoked sausages
½ c. brown sugar, packed

Cut bacon slices in half and arrange on an ungreased baking sheet. Bake at 350 degrees for about 20 minutes, or until cooked but not crisp. Remove from oven; cool slightly and drain. Wrap each mini sausage in a bacon slice; secure with wooden toothpicks. Return to baking sheet and sprinkle with brown sugar. Bake, uncovered, at 350 degrees for about 20 minutes, until bacon is crisp. Makes about 3½ dozen.

Knuckle Tips

Fried Bones

Fried Bones

These little treats are crunchy and good!

16-oz. pkg. egg roll wrappers
1 doz. pieces string cheese
8-oz. can pizza sauce
8-oz. pkg. sliced pepperoni
oil for deep frying

Lay out egg roll wrappers on a counter. Top each wrapper with a piece of string cheese, 2 tablespoons pizza sauce and 4 pepperoni slices. Roll up, tucking in the sides as you roll. In a deep fryer over high heat, heat several inches of oil to 375 degrees. Add egg rolls, a few at a time. Cook for 2 to 3 minutes, or until golden. Remove with a slotted spoon. Drain on paper towels; let cool before serving. Makes one dozen.

HALLOWEEN TIP
Try adding your own favorite goodies to these egg rolls. Why not add a little chopped cabbage or finely chopped ham instead of the pepperoni?

Chapter 7

Gooseberry Grab Bag

(How-You-Make-It Information)

Making spooktacular Halloween projects isn't a mystery at all when you have instructions and patterns to help you along the way! So grab your craft supplies and get in the spirit to make the projects you love. All you need to know is right here!

Limbs & Organs Centerpiece/ Body Parts Plates
(shown on page 28)
MATERIALS:
- clear glass fish bowls, plates, glasses or other clear glass item
- decoupage medium or glue mixture (3 parts water to one part white crafts glue)
- paintbrush
- soft wet cloth

DIRECTIONS:
1. **For the centerpieces,** be sure the glass is clean and dry. Copy and cut out the desired label, page 190. Spread the glue mixture on the *wrong* side of the label and carefully press onto the bowl, working any wrinkles from the paper. Carefully brush another coat of decoupage medium over the front of the label just past the cut edge, wiping any excess with the wet cloth.
2. **For the plates,** apply the mixture to the *right* side of the art. Place on the back side of the dishes. Carefully brush another coat of decoupage medium over the art just past the cut edge, wiping any excess with the wet cloth. Allow to dry.
   Note: Dishes are not washable on the side where the paper has been placed.

Rattle-Me-Bones Place Cards
(shown on page 33)
MATERIALS:
- small plastic bones (3 for each holder)
- satin craft paint: gray and ivory
- small foam paint brush
- scraps of colorful cardstock papers
- 1³⁄₈" foil adhesive letters
- hot-glue gun and glue sticks

DIRECTIONS:
1. Paint bones with gray craft paint and let dry. Paint ivory paint over gray bones, wiping paint over shapes to leave some gray areas. Let paint dry. Glue 3 bones together in an "A" shape.
2. Trace pattern, page 193, for frame backing onto colored cardstock paper. Fold along top and bottom fold lines. Glue frame backing onto back edges of bone frame.
3. Cut rectangular shape from colored cardstock paper. Adhere initial letter to center of paper and place on frame.

Them Bones Table
(shown on page 33)
MATERIALS:
- beveled oval-shaped wooden piece for top
- foam or plastic bone shapes about 12" long
- small plastic bone shapes for trim
- gray satin craft paint
- ivory satin craft paint
- small foam paintbrush
- clear sealer finish
- hot-glue gun and glue sticks
- strong glue, such as Gorilla Glue

DIRECTIONS:
1. Paint wood piece with gray paint and let dry. Paint ivory paint over the gray, streaking paint to allow some of the gray to show through. Paint bone pieces in same style. Brush clear sealer finish over top of table; let dry.
2. Cut top of long bone pieces so they have flat level ends. Measure sections so they are the same length and adjust accordingly. Using strong glue, adhere bone leg pieces to bottom side of oval wood piece. Put large book or other weight on top to help glue set in place. Let dry overnight.
3. Glue small bone pieces around outside edge of tabletop, overlapping shapes in random fashion.

Black Boa Tarantulas
(shown on page 37)
Small spider dimensions: 6" w x 4" h
Large spider dimensions: 12" w x 5½" h
MATERIALS:
- black chenille stems
- black feathered boa
- silver pony beads
- hot-glue gun and glue sticks
- scissors

DIRECTIONS:
To make the small spider:
1. Form the body by grabbing 8 chenille stems and twisting the middle section together to form the spider body. Separate the legs into groups of 2 making a total of 8 legs.
2. Slide a single pony bead onto each pair of chenille stems. Position the beads halfway up the legs. Fold one stem end from each pair back to the body. Wrap the end around

continued on page 174

continued from page 173

its mate alongside the body twist. You'll now have formed 8 fat thighs with pony bead knees. Slide a second bead onto the 8 remaining single chenille stems. Fold 1" of each stem end up to make double-thick feet. The beads should rest just above the folded chenille end.

3. Use one last chenille stem to make a pair of feelers that emerge from the body. Find the center of the stem and fold both ends into the middle. Position the center in the back of the spiders body and weave the 2 feelers through the thighs until they protrude out the front. Twist them once to lock them around the body, then let the folded ends stick straight out.

4. Finally, cut off a 5" section of feathered boa, tie it in a loose knot and hot-glue it to the top of the body.

To make the big spider:

1. For the body, grasp 12 chenille stems in each hand. Connect the 2 groupings by twisting the last 2" of the stems together. The twisted connection will be the spider body; the chenille stem ends will become the legs.

2. Each spider leg is made from 3 chenille stems. Thread a pony bead onto each 3-stem grouping, sliding the bead halfway up the length of the legs. Fold back one of the 3 legs and wrap the end around one of its mates alongside the twisted body. (This step holds the bead in place and thickens the spiders thigh.) Repeat the process with the 7 remaining groups. Slide another bead onto each of the legs, which have now been reduced to 2 stems. Fold up the bottom 1½" of the stem ends and let them rest just below the second bead. This will give the spider firmer footing and hold the second bead in place.

3. Make the feelers by using a single chenille stem and folding it down 1½" on either end. Place the single thickness middle of the stem in the back of the spider body. Weave the folded ends through the legs until they emerge out the front, twist them once to lock them around the body then let the folded ends stick straight out. Cut a 7" section of feathered boa and tie it in a loose knot. Hot-glue it over the top of the twisted body.

Bloodcurdling Candles & Candlesticks
(shown on page 37)

MATERIALS:
- black wood candlesticks
- off-white spray paint
- black dimensional paint
- taper candle
- white pillar candlesticks
- red crayons

DIRECTIONS:

1. Working in a well-ventilated area over newspapers, paint the purchased candlestick with a light spray of white paint. Let the spray paint dry completely.

2. Using black dimensional paint, squeeze onto the candlestick. Paint the spiders coming from different directions up the base but all heading towards the candle at the top.

3. Working over a protected area, and with flammable objects out of reach, hold the end of long red crayon in your fingertips over the white pillar candle. Light the taper candle and melt the red crayon allowing the drips to form on the pillar candle. Once the crayon is warmed it will continue to drip very quickly. As the crayon gets smaller, start with a new crayon. Let the candle harden completely before moving it.

Hallo-Wees
(shown on pages 40–41)

MATERIALS:
- wool roving in suggested colors
- 36 gauge needle felting tool
- foam pad work surface

DIRECTIONS:

General needle-felting instructions for all projects:
Roll portion of wool in between palm of hands. (This efficiently compacts the wool.) Using an all-purpose felting needle and foam pad work surface, push the needle repeatedly through the fibers to shape the wool. It helps to hold the wool in place with one needle, and use another needle for shaping. Keep in mind that the portion of wool roving you pull out will reduce in size by at least half after you've finished felting it.

For Gideon Ghost & Pete Punkin,
colors needed: black, creme, pink, orange, green

1. Roll a bit of creme wool between palm of hands. (See Photo A.) Then create a conical shape out of creme roving, round the top, and spread the bottom out with felting needle for the ghost's body. (See Photo B.)
2. Create two smaller conical shapes out of creme for arms. (See Photos C and D.)
3. Felt, and attach to sides of ghost. (See Photos E and F.)
4. Add pink ball for nose. Use black for eyes, brows and mouth. (See Photos G and H.)

For Little Pete Punkin: Roll a bit of orange wool into ball, felt until compact. Add tiny eyes and mouth with black felt, roll tubular tiny shape out of green wool for stem; attach. Then attach completed pumpkin to ghost's arm.

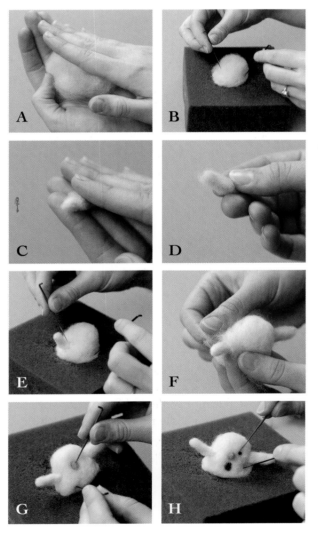

For Franklin-stein, *colors needed: green, charcoal, purple, light brown, dark brown, pink, black*

1. Create 2 tubular shapes for the shirt and pants using purple. Connect shirt and pants by pushing the needle through both layers all the way around his "waist". Use the felting needle to add definition. Create smaller tubular shapes from purple for the arms. Use a tiny bit of green for each hand; attach to the purple arms. Attach arms/hands to his shirt/body. The dark brown wool shoes are felted first, then attached to the pants/body. Use the needle to add definition to the center of the shoes.
2. For the head, use the green wool; attach head to top of body. Add small bits of charcoal felt for hair, eyes, mouth, neck bolts and forehead jag. Drag the tip of the felting needle across his hair to create tiny arcs. For mouth, roll a tiny bit of charcoal in between the fingers, so it is a long, skinny piece, about ½" long. Using the point of the needle on one side of his smile, poke through both layers to attach, then use the needle along his smile to carefully attach. Use a tiny ball of pink for his nose and for the eyes.

For Franklin's Bride, *colors needed: charcoal, creme, peach, red, pink, black*

1. Create a long tubular shape for her dress out of the creme roving. Use the needle along the bottom edge of her dress to pull the fibers out, all the way around, creating a "ruffle" detail on her dress.
2. For arms, create 2 tubular shapes out of the peach roving, rolling between fingers first. Attach to dress/body.
3. For the head create a ball using peach; attach to dress/body. Use charcoal wool to attach hair to her head. Keep the wool for her hair loose. For the white streaks, take some of the creme wool, roll between fingers, then attach to sides of hair with the needle, start with bottom point and attach at different points moving up into her hair, in a sort of zigzag pattern to get the swirl look. Add a small bit of red for top and bottom of lips, a tiny ball of pink for nose and a tiny bit of black for eyes.

continued on page 176

continued from page 175

For Mini Mummy, *colors needed: black, creme, pink*

1. With creme wool, create tubular shape for body, legs, arms and ball for head. Attach, with arms jutting straight out. Needle felt strips of creme to wrap around mummy body. Roll creme felt between fingers, then wrap around him at different angles. Use the charcoal wool to "outline" the wrappings, just on one side of each strip. Add the black mouth, one black eye and small ball of pink for nose.

For Witch Hazel, *colors needed: purple, gold, red, peach, pink, black*

1. Create a triangular shape out of the black wool for the witch's body/dress. Create tubular shapes for arms out of black wool. Create balls of peach for her hands. Attach hands to arms, and then attach each arm/hand to her body/dress.
2. For the head, make an oval shape out of peach and add a tiny bit for a pointy chin for her face. Attach to body/dress. Add red hair, letting the roving stay loose. Create a conical shape out of black roving. Add in the rim of the hat. Using purple wool rolled between fingers, wrap around base of hat and felt through fibers to attach. Add tiny rolled gold roving fibers for buckle.
3. **For broom,** glue cut raffia to the top of a tiny stick such as a part of a toothpick. Tie with black embroidery floss.

For Lil' Count, *colors needed: black, crimson, light grey, creme, pink*

1. Create body, shoes and arms from tubular shapes using black. Use grey for hands; attach to arms. Add creme sleeve detail. Attach arms to body. Add tiny bit of grey for buttons on shirt front, creme roving for collar and black for bow-tie.
2. Create the head from grey roving, starting with a ball. Add hair, brows, eyes and smile with black. Make teeth using creme, using tiny bits rolled and shaped to a point. Attach to bottom of smile. Shape the hair to a point with felting needle.
3. **For cape,** create 2 pieces: a larger black trapezoidal-shape for the bottom, and a smaller trapezoidal-shape for the top. Line with crimson by spreading the crimson roving thin, and attach in a thin layer. Once the cape

pieces are felted and attached to each other, attach to back of the figure.

Ghostly Duo
(shown on page 39)

MATERIALS:
- wide white muslin or white sheet
- bottle of liquid fabric starch
- rose cone form
- ball (soccer or smaller basketball)
- wood dowel sticks
- newspapers
- 12"x 12" black felt square
- marking pencil
- crafts glue

DIRECTIONS:

1. Cover surface with newspapers. Stack ball on top of rose cone. (This will be the form for draping the fabric over to make a ghost shape.) Cut or rip fabric into a length that is sufficient to cover cone/ball form, at least one yard of 90" w fabric, depending on size of cone and ball. Arrange fabric over form to get an idea of how you want the ghost to look, pulling out sides to make arms.
2. Dip fabric into full strength fabric starch, working starch into fabric with your hands and squeezing out some of the excess. Drape wet fabric over the cone/ball shape, stretching out ends to make desired shape. Prop wooden dowel sticks under fabric to lift it up for arm shapes. Let fabric dry for 24 hours until stiff and dry.
3. Enlarge and trace eye, eyebrow and mouth pieces, page 189, onto tracing paper and cut out. Pin patterns onto black felt and cut out. Glue facial features onto heads of ghost shapes. Let dry.

Scarecrow Couple
(shown on page 38)

MATERIALS:
- three 5-ft. garden stakes (1½ for each scarecrow)
- twine or packing string
- assorted discarded clothes
- safety pins
- carvable plastic pumpkin for head (6" to 8" diameter for life-size head)
- straw hat or handkerchief for head covering
- newspapers for stuffing
- loose straw
- desired accessories

DIRECTIONS:

1. To make form for scarecrow, latch together 2 garden stakes in a cross shape with shorter one crossing over larger one. For outstretched arms like the male scarecrow, use a horizontal stake about 3½ ft. long. For arms down like the female scarecrow, use a horizontal stake about 1½ ft. long. Place horizontal stake about 7" below the top of the vertical stake. Use twine or string to tie the pieces snuggly together.

2. Dress scarecrow in desired clothes. Stuff form with crumpled newspapers. Pin bottom of shirts together with safety pins to hold newspapers in place. Tie twine around pant legs and sleeve ends to keep stuffing in place. Stuff a small amount of straw at ends of arms, legs and at neck edge.

3. Carve faces into artificial pumpkins, using sharp paring knife or other cutting tool. Place pumpkin head on top of dressed, stuffed form. Add hat, head scarf, bandanna, basket or other desired accessories.

Party Invitations

Haunted Open House Invitation:
(shown on page 44)
MATERIALS:
- black, white and gold/yellow cardstock
- black or charcoal ink for edging and shading
- black marker
- one black mini brad
- piercing tool
- circle cutter or template
- scissors
- adhesive, including fine tipped liquid glue
- computer/printer for creating text
- A2 size envelope
- matching paper and cardstock
- small stamp and black ink
- circle punch
- die cut shape or label
- scoring tool

DIRECTIONS:

1. Trace haunted house pattern, page 192, onto black cardstock and cut out. To create the full moon, cut a 4" circle from gold/yellow cardstock and ink the edges. Adhere the haunted house to the front of the moon.

2. Create invitation text on the computer to fit across front of invitation. Cut out roughly, ink and adhere as shown. Print text to fit inside a 4" circle on scrap paper. Cut text into a 4" circle to fit behind moon.

3. Use a piercing tool to make a hole through the invitation, moon and circular text piece. Insert brad through all 3 layers. Rotate text piece of invitation to check placement. Adjust spacing on the computer as needed, then print final piece on white cardstock.

4. Freehand cut small windows and door from gold/yellow cardstock. Use a black marker to draw panes on windows. Ink each piece and adhere to the invitation using fine-tipped liquid glue. Cut a small bat from black cardstock and adhere to the moon.

5. **For the envelope,** ink the outside edges of the envelope. Cut a piece of matching paper to fit inside the envelope; score at fold. Adhere to inside of envelope. Cut a label piece to fit the front of the envelope. Ink and adhere securely to front. Stamp image onto matching cardstock; punch with circle punch. Ink and adhere as a seal to the completed invitation.

Sinfully Sensational Soup Supper Invitation:
(shown on page 58)
MATERIALS:
- black and 3 shades of green cardstock
- circle punches: ⅛", ½", ¾"
- fine-tipped glitter glue or self-adhesive gems
- embossing tool
- trimmer and scissors
- adhesive, including foam dots
- computer/printer for creating text

DIRECTIONS:

1. Trace cauldron pattern, page 193; set aside. Cut a rectangle of black cardstock to fit inside the envelope. Create invitation text on a slightly smaller piece of light green cardstock, leaving space at the bottom for the cauldron.

2. Create text piece on green and adhere to black cardstock. Trace pattern onto black cardstock; cut out. Emboss the body of the cauldron to add texture. Adhere the cauldron to the lower portion of the invitation using foam dots.

3. Punch circles of various sizes and shades of green to create bubbles. Arrange some bubbles inside the cauldron by slipping them

continued on page 178

continued from page 177

below the top edge and adhering them in place. Adhere other bubbles to the front of the cauldron and elsewhere on the invitation. Use foam dots behind some for added dimension. Add a few dots of glitter glue to some of the bubbles for sparkle.

Little Monster Bash Invitation:

(shown on page 68)

MATERIALS:

- white, orange and black cardstock
- striped paper to match cardstock
- glossy photo paper
- large googly eye
- craft thread or floss
- small hole punch
- corner rounder
- trimmer
- scissors
- adhesive, including fine-tipped liquid glue and foam dots
- computer/printer for creating text
- white envelope
- mist spray, such as Glimmer Mist in matching color
- white cardstock for label
- small sticker
- paper for lining envelope

DIRECTIONS:

1. Trace monster pattern, page 192; set aside. Cut white cardstock to $4\frac{1}{4}$" x $5\frac{1}{2}$". Round 2 right corners. Print text pieces on glossy photo paper and cut to fit invitation. Adhere to left portion of white cardstock. Adhere strip of striped paper across bottom of invitation, rounding corner.
2. Trace monster onto orange cardstock and cut out. Create and print a small "Boo" tag; trim corners and punch small hole in top. Wrap thread around monster's waist, then thread tag onto floss and tie bow. Use a small dot of liquid glue beneath bow to hold it in place.
3. Adhere monster to card with foam dots. Adhere googly eye using liquid glue. Cut a narrow strip of black cardstock for a mouth and adhere to monster. Cut 2 triangle teeth from glossy photo paper and adhere just below mouth.
4. **For the envelope,** lightly spray the envelope with glitter mist for a spattered look. Allow to dry. Cut a piece of matching paper to fit inside the envelope; score at fold. Adhere

paper to inside of envelope. Create a label for the outside of the envelope, incorporating sticker. Glue sticker to label; glue label to front of envelope.

Scary Movie Countdown Invitation:

(shown on page 82)

MATERIALS:

- white cardstock
- glossy photo paper
- trimmer
- adhesive
- black/charcoal ink for aging invitation
- computer/printer for generating text

DIRECTIONS:

1. Copy printed filmstrip, page 192, onto glossy photo paper and cut out. Create text to fit 5"x 7" invitation, leaving room for filmstrip at the top.
2. Create "ticket" at bottom of invitation by indicating a cutting line just above ticket. Ink the edges of the invitation. Adhere filmstrip to top portion of invitation.
   Note: The ticket portion can also be used as an RSVP to the party.

Ghostly Cookie Caper Invitation:

(shown on page 94)

MATERIALS:

- small box with lid
- patterned paper and matching cardstock
- trimmer and scissors
- scoring tool
- adhesive, including foam dots
- fine-tipped dimensional paint, such as Liquid Pearls
- shredded paper filling
- ribbon
- cookie cutter
- cookie recipe
- computer/printer for generating text

DIRECTIONS:

1. Cover outside and inside of box with cardstock and patterned paper. Place a folded bit of ribbon on lid to create a loop for opening. Cover cut ends of ribbon with paper or cardstock.
2. **For the invitation,** cut cardstock to make invitation which will fit inside box. Score to fold. Create text for front and inside of invitation. Add a drawing of a ghost or copyright-free clip art of a ghost.

3. Add cardstock strips to front of invitation; adhere text to front using foam dots. Adhere text to inside of invitation. Add dimensional paint accents to front of invitation as desired; allow to dry.
4. Print recipe on lightweight cardstock or paper; roll and tie with ribbon. Tie ribbon to cookie cutter. Place filler in box; add invitation, cookie cutter and recipe. Wrap box to mail or deliver in person.

All Hallow's Eve Feast Invitation:
(shown on page 106)
MATERIALS:
• black and cream cardstock
• trimmer
• fine-tipped scissors
• adhesive, including small foam dots
• fine-tipped dimensional paint, such as Liquid Pearls in black/dark gray
• computer/printer for generating text

DIRECTIONS:
1. Trace candelabra pattern, page 193, onto black cardstock and cut out using fine-tipped scissors. Cut a rectangle from black cardstock to fit inside the envelope.
2. Create text box, allowing space for candelabra at bottom. Print final copy onto cream cardstock, then mat onto black.
3. Adhere the candelabra to the lower left of the invitation using foam dots. Add dots of dimensional paint as desired. Allow to dry.

Countess of Chocolate Invitation:
(shown on page 118)
MATERIALS:
• chocolate bar which has both a paper and foil wrapper
• dark brown and cream cardstock
• brown tulle
• scoring tool
• trimmer
• scissors
• adhesive, including strong tape adhesive, such as Tacky Tape
• pencil
• computer/printer for creating text

DIRECTIONS:
1. Remove paper wrapper from the candy bar, leaving the foil wrapper in place. Cut a piece of brown cardstock in the same size as the paper wrapper. Lightly bend the cardstock around the candy bar, marking the sides of the bar with a pencil on the back side. Score edges and fold so that cardstock extends smoothly around the candy bar. Tape backside of cardstock with strong tape adhesive.
2. Create text for the invitation on the computer, incorporating desired image on left. Print on cream cardstock. Adhere invitation to top of candy bar with tape adhesive. Tie tulle around candy bar.
Note: Hand deliver this invitation, or mail it in a padded envelope or small box with filler.

Night-Owl
(shown on page 148)
Shown Size: 3T-4T
MATERIALS:
• orange tan or brown sweatshirt with or without zipper in desired size
• brown fleece hat
• nonwoven felt, such as National Nonwoven's: one yard *each* of tan, light brown, dark brown, ½ yard *each* of light pink and purple, scrap of orange
• 2 large buttons
• brown embroidery floss
• off-white machine quilting thread
• sewing machine
• sewing and embroidery needle
• scissors

DIRECTIONS:
1. Enlarge and trace patterns, pages 199–201.
Note: Cut all the feathered chest pieces to template size. If you're using a solid front shirt, extend the feather pattern to stretch across the entire width of the chest without breaks. Adjust the length of the wing pieces to fit the sleeve of your sweatshirt. Outstretch the sleeve over the wing pattern, lengthen or shorten the pattern until it stretches from the shoulder to the cuff.

Cut the following felt pieces:
• 2 top feathered chest pieces from tan felt
• multiple feathered chest pieces, alternate between the 2 different patterns and cut from the tan, light pink and purple felt.

continued on page 180

- 2 outer wings out of dark brown
- 2 inner wings out of light brown
- 2 large eyes out of tan
- 2 large eyes out of light brown
- 2 medium eyes out of purple
- 2 small eyes out of beige
- 2 inset eyes out of dark brown

2. The top feathered chest pieces should fit around the shoulder seam and collar of the sweatshirt. Tuck the top edge of the feathered chest pieces under the bottom edge of the top feathered chest piece. Keep adding feathered chest pieces alternating between the 2 patterns while establishing a repeating color pattern. Once you've covered the front of the shirt, carefully lift up the feathered edges and pin the straight edges to the sweatshirt.

3. If using a shirt with zipper, unzip the sweatshirt and machine stitch the straight top edges of all the feathered chest pieces in place, pinning the feathered ends out of the way. Once all the pieces are sewn in place, trim any felt that extends beyond the sides seams of the shirt.

4. Stack a light brown front wing over a dark brown back wing. Pin the top edge together and then machine stitch. Turn the connected wing right side out.

5. Outstretch the shirt sleeves. Lay a connected wing over each sleeve. The brown back wing should fall over the back of the sleeve and the light brown over the front of the sleeve. Pin the wings to the sleeve. Hand stitch the seamed wing connection down the center of each sleeve. The feathered edges should hang loose. Hand stitch the inside edge of the front wing to sweatshirt sleeve/armhole connection. Hand stitch the shoulder area of the back wing to the back of the sweatshirt.

6. **For hat**, working from biggest to smallest pieces, stack the eye pieces together. Pin each eye stack close together on the hat, they'll separate when the fabric stretches during wear. Place a button over the smallest felt circle. Draw a full strand of embroidery floss up from inside of the hat and out through a button hole. Sew back down through the button; repeat. This single connection will anchor all the eyepieces to the hat. Repeat the process to stitch the other eyepieces and

button in place. Tuck the beak between the eyes and make a single stitch across the top to hold it in place.

Little Miss Mermaid
(shown on page 150)

Shown Size: 3-6 months

MATERIALS

- white long sleeved onesie
- ½ yard woven striped fabric
- nonwoven felt, such as National Nonwoven's: ½ yard medium blue, scraps light blue and pink
- ½" w elastic cording
- purchased pink baby cap
- off-white and blue sewing thread
- sewing machine
- sewing needles
- scissors

DIRECTIONS:

1. Enlarge and trace patterns, page 198.
   Note: Add a ¼" seam allowance to the fabric skirt pattern and the large tailpieces. Do not add a seam allowance to the decorative tail inset.

Cut the following pieces:

- 2 large tailpieces from medium blue felt
- 2 small tail inserts from pink felt
- 2 skirt pieces from the striped fabric
- 2 large shells from pink felt
- 2 medium shells from light blue felt
- 2 small shell inserts from medium blue felt

2. Lay the light blue tail inserts over the medium blue tails, stitch them in place. Placing right sides together, lay a finished tail over the end of each skirt piece. Machine stitch a felt tail to the bottom of each skirt piece. Open and flatten the tail pieces to check seams.

3. Placing right sides together, stack the 2 tail pieces together. Pin the sides together and then stitch down each side of the skirt leaving the felt tail piece unsewn. Turn the tail right side out. Line up the edges of the 2 felt tail pieces, pin them together. Top stitch around the outside edge of the felt tail pieces.

4. Turn the tail inside out. Working along the waist, fold down 1" (skirt) fabric. Pin the folded fabric in place.

5. Make a seam ¾" from the fold to create a channel for the elastic waist. Leave a small 1" opening between the beginning and end of the seam. Attach a safety pin to the end of the elastic. Insert the safety pin into the channel and push the safety pin through the channel. Bring the elastic ends together, adjusting the length of the elastic to fit your child.
   Tip: Use a pair of elastic waist pants that fit your child as a visual guide to gauge the elastic length. Tie the elastic ends in an overhand knot.

6. **For the onesie bikini,** stack a light blue shell over each pink shell, then top the light blue shells with a dark blue insert. Pin the stacked felt pieces together. Machine stitch the shell pieces together. Stitch around the inside edge of the dark blue shell insert and then around the outside edge of the light blue shell. Hand stitch the finished shells to the onesie.

7. **For the hat,** cut freeform star shapes from felt scraps. Layer the felt pieces and add a small piece of white tulle at the center. Attach to purchased hat with a few hand stitches.

A Little Squirrelly
(shown on page 151)
Shown Size: 3T
MATERIALS:
- hooded sweatshirt
- fleece hat
- fleece mittens
- one yard white fun fur
- one yard grey fun fur
- scraps of grey felt
- polyester fiberfill
- sewing thread
- sewing machine
- scissors
- sewing needle
- hot-glue gun and glue sticks

DIRECTIONS:
1. Enlarge and trace patterns, pages 202–203.
   Note: Don't add a seam allowance to the templates, cut to the actual size. Be sure to reverse the patterns as indicated.

Cut the following pieces:
- one tail from white fur and one tail from gray fur, reversing the pattern so the tail pieces are opposite.
- 2 front chest pieces out of white fur, reversing the pattern so they are mirror images of each other.
- 2 ears out of white fur and 2 ears out of gray fur
- 2 gray mitten backs–trace mittens to determine size
- six 1" gray felt circles for the mittens
- two 1" x 2" gray felt ovals for the mittens

2. Lay the yoke piece over the back of the sweatshirt, lining it up with the neckline and shoulder seams; pin in place. Flip the shirt over and position the front chest pieces on either side, lining up each piece with shirt shoulder seams neckline center opening; pin in place. Machine stitch around the outside edge of all 3 pieces to attach to the shirt.

3. **For the tail,** stack the gray and white fur tail pieces right sides together. Machine stitch around the outside edge leaving a 3-inch opening at the base. Pull the tail right side out through the opening. Pull out any fluff that is stuck in the seam. Push stuffing into the opening, filling the top third of the tail and then loosely stuffing the bottom half.
   Note: An over-stuffed tail will be too heavy and cumbersome for the shirt to support.

4. Position the tail over the back of the sweatshirt. Hand stitch the opening closed and then start hand stitching the underside of the tail to the back of the sweatshirt. Leave the top third of the tail unattached and sew back down the other side of the tail to firmly anchor it to the shirt.

5. Placing right sides together, pair the gray and white fur ears together. Machine stitch the outside edge of each pair of ears, leaving the bottom unattached. Pull the ears right side out through the bottom opening. Pull out any trapped fur. Position the ears towards the front of the fleece hat and hand stitch the open base closed while attaching them to either side of the hat. Rip a 2"x12" section of white fur and fold it around the front edge of the hat; machine stitch in place.

6. Hand stitch the gray fur over the back of each white mitten. Turn the mittens over and hot-glue felt circles to the end of each thumb, and two circles to the finger tips. Glue the oval over the palm area.

Just-for-Me Princess Costumes

(shown on page 152)

Costume Sizing: A 20" waist should fit most children 2 to 5 years old. Test-fit the elastic around your child before cutting and stitching it together.

MATERIALS:

For skirts:

- 6" rolls of tulle in the following colors:
  2 orange, 2 yellow, one white (Candy Corn)
  2 dark pink, 2 light pink, one white and one bright green (Strawberry)
  3 dark aqua, 3 light aqua (Butterfly)
- spools of ribbon in the following colors:
  2 spools of yellow dotted orange ribbon, one spool each of yellow and orange sheer (Candy Corn)
  one spool pink satin, one spool of dark pink sheer (Strawberry) one spool blue satin (Butterfly)
- one yard or 20" of 1" w non-roll waistband
- 22 small and 3 large feathered butterflies (Butterfly)
- white pom-poms (Strawberry)

For headbands:

- satin bridal headbands
- white air dry clay, such as Crayola Model Magic (Strawberry and Candy Corn)
- acrylic paint: fuchsia pink and dimensional white (Strawberry)/ white, yellow and white (Candy Corn)
- 5 small and 2 large feathered butterflies (Butterfly)

For wands:

- colored foam sheets, such as Fun Foam
- flexible wand sticks
- ribbon
- adhesive jewels
- glitter
- crafts glue

Tools:

- scissors
- rotary cutter, mat and clear ruler
- hot-glue gun and glue sticks
- wire cutters

DIRECTIONS:

For the Skirts:

1. To form the tutu waistband, loop the 20" length of non-roll elastic, overlap the ends and stitch them together. Working over the cutting mat, with the ruler and rotary cutter, cut the rolls of tulle into 24" lengths.
2. To attach the strips to the waistband, first fold the tulle in half, then slide the loop up into the waistband. Bring the tulle ends up around the outside of the elastic then thread them through the loop. Pull the length of the strip ends out until a knot forms around the waistband.
3. Continue adding strips in the following sequences:

For the Candy Corn: Group the colors together to make bold sections of color. Tie 6 white tulle strips around the waistband then 6 yellow and 6 orange. Repeat the sequence until you've tightly encircled the waistband. Cut the polka dot ribbon into 12" lengths and tie the center of each ribbon around the waistband, push the tulle to the sides to fit it in-between. Position the ribbon 2" to 3" apart. Trim the ribbon ends into tidy points and let them fall over the tulle.

For the Strawberry: Strawberries are mixed with light and dark sections. To create this effect tie the following sequence around the waistband: 3 dark pinks, 2 light pink, one white, 2 pink, repeat. Cut the green tulle into 16" lengths trimming the ends on the diagonal. Fold and tie these leaf sections around the waistband align them with the dark pink tulle. Cut the pink satin ribbon into 12" lengths and tie the center of each ribbon around the waistband, push the tulle to the sides to fit in-between. Position the ribbon at each white section. Trim the ribbon ends into tidy points and let them fall over the tulle. Hot-glue a scattering of small white pom-poms over the top of the tutu.

For the Butterfly: For a shimmering blue effect, alternate between light and dark aqua tulle strips around the waistband. Cut the satin ribbon into 12" lengths and tie the center of the ribbon around the waistband at 2" to 3" intervals. Use wire cutters to trim the butterfly wires to 1" long. Poke the wire into the tulle and then fold it back against the butterfly's body. Use a dab of hot glue to anchor it in place. Repeat the process to scatter butterflies all over the tutu.

Note: To keep your tutu in tip-top condition, use your fingers to comb the strips smooth. For added stability make a continuous seam through the tulle knots right below the elastic.

For the Headbands:

1. Mold the strawberries or candy corn out of

the air dry clay. Pinch off a piece and roll an oversized 2"x1" strawberry or candy corn shape. You'll need 4 to 6 pieces for each headband. Let pieces dry overnight, turning them to release trapped moisture on the underside.

2. Working over wax paper, brush the acrylic paint onto the dried clay to transform it into candy or fruit. The widest part of the corn is orange, the middle yellow and the top white. The darkest part of the strawberries is reddish pink and it lightens to pink at the bottom. Add small white dot seeds over the finished strawberries. Let the paint dry.

3. Cut the ribbons into 12" lengths. Then wrap around the headband just like the tulle strips wrapped around the waistband. Fold a ribbon length in half, place the loop under the headband, wrap the ends around the headband then pull them out through the loop. Pull tight and trim the ribbon ends into sharp points. Cover the crown of the headband with ribbons. **For the Strawberry Headband,** alternate between the light and dark sheer pink ribbons. **For the Candy Corn Headband,** punctuate the orange and yellow sheer ribbons with a section of the polka dot ribbon.

4. **For the Strawberry Headband,** hot-glue small pieces of green tulle to band for leaves. Hot-glue finished strawberries across the top of the headband, anchoring them over the tied ribbons and leaves.

5. **For the Candy Corn Headband,** hot-glue finished candy corn across the top of the headband, over orange and yellow ribbons.

6. **For the Butterfly Headband,** wrap the wires attached to a few of the small butterflies around the headband, letting them flutter 1" to 3" above the headband. Peel off the clip and hot-glue the base of the large butterflies

directly to the headband. Remove the wires from a few small butterflies and hot-glue them to the headband.

For the Wands:
1. Trace patterns, page 194; cut out. Trace onto foam sheets making two of each desired shape; cut out. Glue wand stick between the shapes. Decorate with jewels and glitter. Tie ribbons under shape.

Halloween Headbands
(shown on pages 154–155)
For the Mummy Bride Headband:
MATERIALS:
- black fabric-covered headband
- white burlap
- red silk roses
- 2 yards off-white pearl strands (sold with bridal supplies in fabric stores)
- black spray paint
- hot-glue gun and glue sticks
- scissors
- wire cutters

DIRECTIONS:
1. Lightly spray paint the roses over newspaper in a well-ventilated area; let dry.
2. Cut the burlap into 1½" to 2" w strips that vary from 18" to 36" long. Fold each strip in half and tie the center in a loose overhand knot. Hot-glue the knot to the crown of the headband. Thread a length of pearls through the center of the knots and add a dab of glue to anchor the center of them to the knot. Use wire cutters to clip the flower heads from the stems. Hot-glue the blooms between the burlap knots.

For the Bones and Roses Topper:
MATERIALS:
- black fabric-covered headband
- one yard of black tulle
- small artificial red rose buds and flowers
- white air-dry clay, such as Crayola Model Magic
- silver and pearl acrylic paint
- sewing thread
- sewing machine or sewing needle
- hot-glue gun and glue sticks
- scissors
- wire cutters

continued on page 184

continued from page 183

DIRECTIONS:

1. Form the clay into 2" to 3½" bones. Let the bones dry flipping them over so that both sides aerate. Brush silver and white paint in the crevices of the bones to make them appear more realistic; let dry.
2. Cut the tulle into 2" wide strips. Fold a section of tulle in half, place the folded loop by the crown of the headband. Wrap the ends around the headband and then pull them through the loop trapping the headband in the tulle. Repeat the process adding strips until the crown of the headband is transformed into a veil.
3. Use wire cutters to remove the rose blooms from the stems. Hot-glue the bones over the tulle covered headband. Use more glue to tuck the roses between the bones.

For the Spider Veil:

MATERIALS:
- black fabric-covered headband
- 1½ yards of white tulle
- black plastic spiders
- pearl trimmed ribbon
- white thread
- sewing machine or sewing needle
- hot-glue gun and glue sticks
- scissors

DIRECTIONS:

1. Machine or hand stitch across the top of one yard of tulle. To gather the tulle, grasp the thread ends, and slide the outer tulle into the center of the threads. Repeat the process with both a 12" and a 6" length of tulle.
2. Hot-glue the gathered edge of the yard-long veil across the headband crown. Then glue the 12" gathered veil over the top of the yard-long veil. Finally glue the 6" veil over the 12" veil. Hot-glue a length of pearl-edged ribbon over the gathered veil edge to conceal the connections.
3. Hot-glue plastic spiders over the ribbon trim and down the length of the all three veil layers. Apply a spot of glue to the underside of the spider and press it down into the tulle, pushing the legs into the openings in the material.

For the Bird on a Branch Headband:

MATERIALS:
- black fabric-covered headband
- thin artificial branches
- feathered bird with metal clip
- black spray paint if painting bird
- hot-glue gun and glue sticks
- wire cutters

DIRECTIONS:

1. Working in a well-ventilated area over a protected surface, spray paint the bird black, and let him dry. Or use black bird.
2. Use wire cutters to cut the more flexible branches off the stiff branches. Cut an assortment of long and short pieces. Clip the bird in place to one side of the headband and then hot-glue the branches around the base of the bird to resemble a perch. Carry the branches down one side of the headband and partially across the top. Select some branches to extend beyond the headband.

For the Witch Hat Headband:

MATERIALS:
- black fabric-covered headband
- feathers
- two 12"x12" stiffened silver-flecked black felt sheets
- black and white striped ribbon
- hot-glue gun and glue sticks
- bowl or plate

DIRECTIONS:

1. Roll one of the felt sheets into a cone shape. Hot-glue the overlapped edge in place. Trim the base of the cone so it stands straight. Find a bowl or plate that is the right size for the base of the hat. Use it as a pattern and trace it onto the second piece of felt. Cut out the circle and then hot-glue the cone to the center.
2. The hat will be placed to one side of the headband crown. Position the feathers so they fan out from under the hat and cascade down the sides. Hot-glue the stiff feather ends to the headband and let the tips sway freely. Keep adding feathers until pleased with the effect.
3. Hot-glue the hat over the feathers, making sure the hat is well secured. Wrap a section of ribbon around the hat and glue it in place.

Terrorific Treat Bags

(shown on page 157)

Skull tote dimensions:17" h x 8.5" w

Cat tote dimensions: 16" h x 8.5" w

MATERIALS

- non-woven wool felt, such as National Nonwovens felt: black, white
- wool felt scraps: green and orange
- embroidery floss: black, green, orange, white
- off-white and black sewing thread
- sewing machine
- sewing and embroidery needle
- scissors

DIRECTIONS:

1. Enlarge and trace patterns, page 197. **Note:** Cut the felt to size, do not add seam allowances.

Cut the following pieces for the cat:

- 4 black cat heads
- 2 black 3" x 22" strips for the gusset
- 4 black 1" x 15½" strips for the handles
- two 1¾" white circles for the outer eye
- two 1½" green circles for the middle eye
- two 1" black circle for the inner eye
- one orange nose
- one orange mouth

Cut the following pieces for the skull:

- 4 white heads
- 2 white 3" x 22″ strips for the gusset
- 4 white 1" x 15½" strips for the handles
- two 1¾" black circles for the outer eye
- two 1½" white circles for the middle eye
- two 1" green circle for the inner eye
- one black nose

2. Separate the felt cat heads into pairs 2 for the front of the tote and 2 for the back. Starting with front cat heads, align one end of the stacked gusset pieces together at the base of the cat ears. The gusset pieces contour the base of the cat head and wrap up to the base of the other ear. Pin the edge of the gusset pieces to the outside edge of the front cat heads. Using black thread, machine stitch all 4 layers of felt together. Place the back cat heads over the back of the tote, lining up the gusset in the identical position as the front. Pin the outside edge of the gusset to the head edge, machine stitch the outside edge together. Pull the tote right side out leaving the side seams hidden inside the bag.

3. Assemble the skull the same way; center the middle of the gusset pieces under the chin, draw the edges up so the end just below the widest part of the head. Switch to off white thread to machine stitch the gusset to the skull pieces.

4. Stack and pin each set of the handle pieces together, machine stitching both sides ⅛" from the outside edge. Center the handles at the top of the front and back of the tote. Slip the last inch of each handle end between the felt layers. Top stitch across the top of head pieces trapping the handle ends in the seams.

5. Stack the eye pieces largest to smallest and pin them to the center of the face. Pin the felt nose and mouth under the eyes, use a sewing needle and thread to hand stitch them in place. Use an embroidery needle and full strand of white floss to make three 1½" to 2" long whiskers on either side of the nose. Each whisker is made with 4 to 5 connected straight stitches. Make a French knot in the center of each black inner eye circle. Then make small decorative stitches that stretch from the outer eye to the head. Switch to a full strand of black floss and blanket stitch around the middle green eye circles. Finally, thread the embroidery needle with a full strand of green floss and make 3 elongated stitches inside each eye.

6. Stack the eye pieces, largest to smallest, and pin them to the center of the face. Pin the felt nose under the eyes. Use an embroidery needle and a full strand of white floss to make small stitches that span from the outer nose to the head. Switch to a full strand of black floss and make 5½" horizontal stitches to form a mouth under the nose. Intersect the mouth stitches with four one-inch vertical stitches. Make a cross-stitch in the center of each green inner eye. Switch to a full strand of orange floss and encircle each of the black outer eyes with a blanket stitch.

7. Thread the embroidery needle with a full strand of black floss and make a decorative straight stitch that contours to the gusset connection, around the sides of the head. When you reach the top of the skull change to blanket stitch. Fill bag with treats.

Haunted House Pumpkin
(page 9)
Size as needed

Pumpkin Faces Size as needed

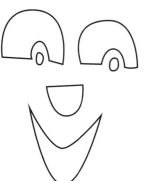

Pumpkin Faces

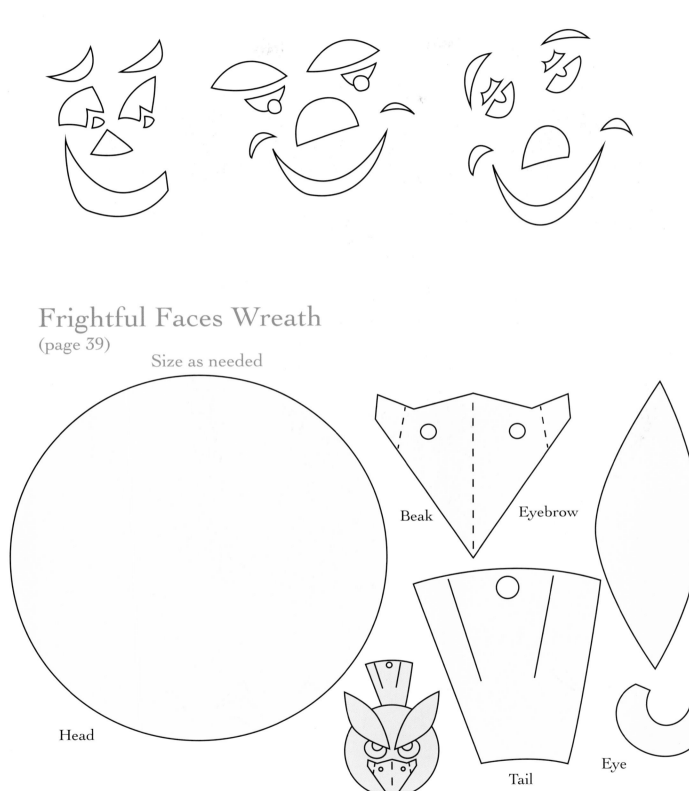

Frightful Faces Wreath
(page 39)

Size as needed

Head

Beak

Eyebrow

Tail

Eye

continued on page 188

Frightful Faces Wreath

(page 39)

Head

Tail

Whiskers

Nose

Eye

Ear

Mouth

Size as needed

Stem

Head

Nose

Eye Parts

Mouth

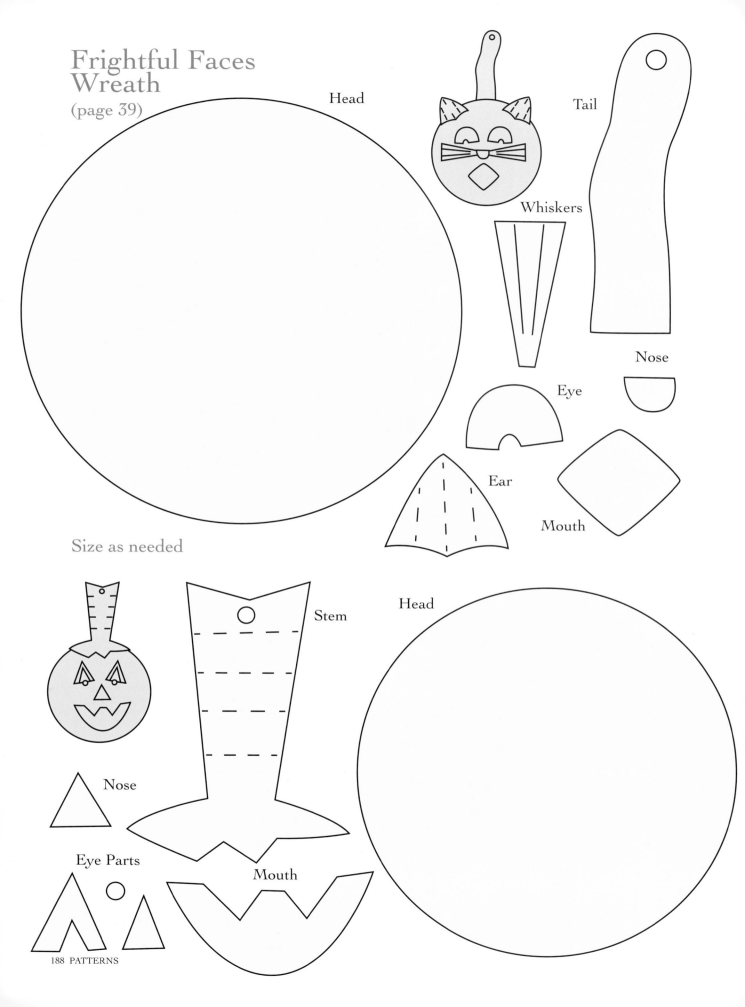

Ghostly Duo
Size as needed
(page 39)

Eyebrow

Eyebrow

Eye

Eye

Mouth

Mouth

Mouth

Cats, Rats & Bats!
(page 12) Size as needed

Limbs & Organs
Centerpieces
(pages 28–31)

STRESS FRACTURED
METATARSAL
BONES
Better then an Achilles Heel
1875

FRESHLY STUBBED
INGROWN
TOENAILS
Clipper Tested Since
1875

ALWAYS TWISTED
PICKLED
INTESTINES
They Go On for Miles
1875

EXTRA LARGE STONES
FLOATING
KIDNEYS
Swamp Water Packed
1875

PUMPED DAILY
BLEEDING
HEARTS
Real to the Last Drop
1875

PRE-WAXED
SEVERED
EARS
Bat Tested, Mummy Approved
1875

FORGET-ME-NOT
BRAINS IN
BRINE
Genius Brain Guaranteed
1875

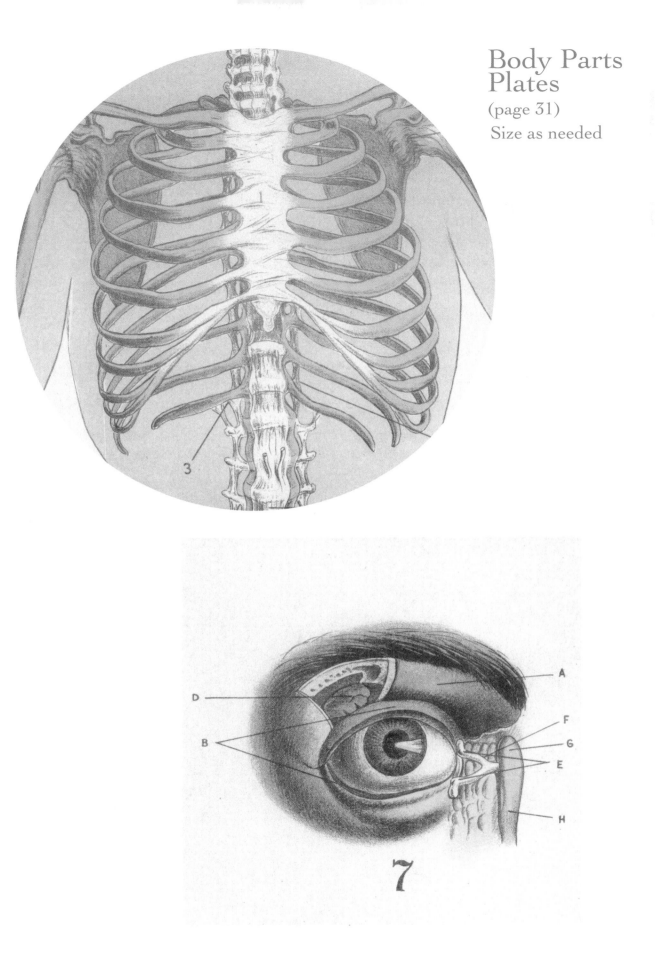

1

3

D

B

A

F

G

E

H

7

Party Invitations

Scary Movie Party
Invitation (page 82)

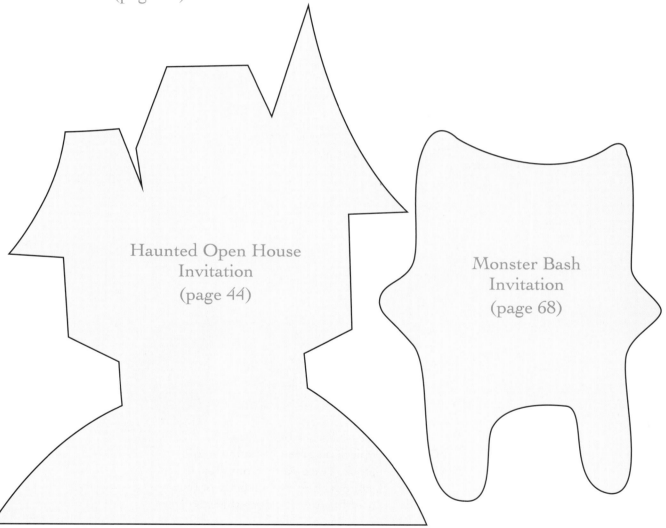

Haunted Open House
Invitation
(page 44)

Monster Bash
Invitation
(page 68)

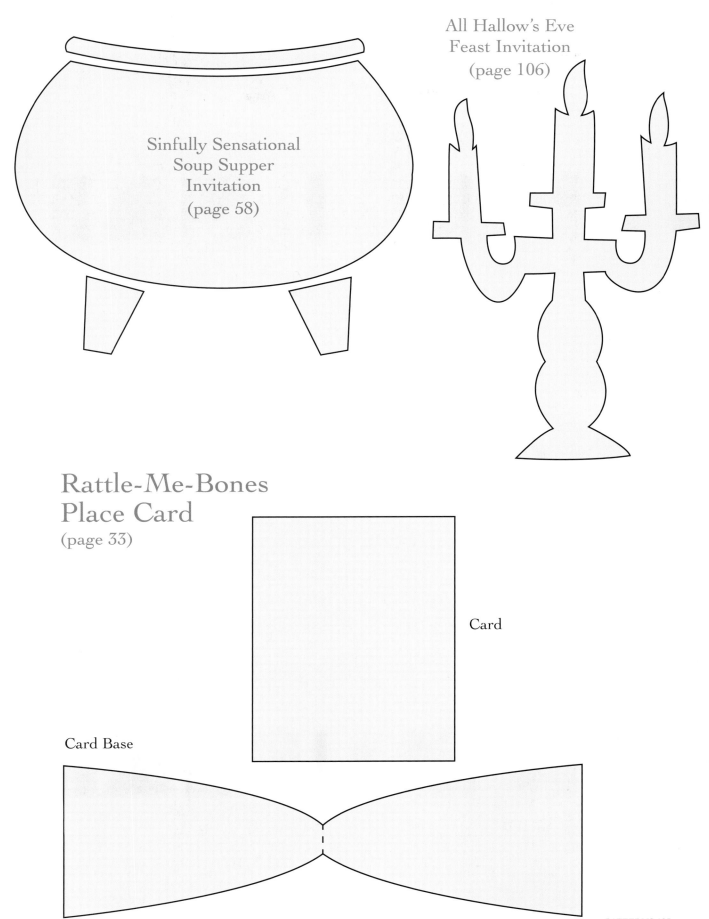

Sinfully Sensational
Soup Supper
Invitation
(page 58)

All Hallow's Eve
Feast Invitation
(page 106)

Rattle-Me-Bones
Place Card
(page 33)

Card

Card Base

Just-for-Me Princess Wands

(page 152)

Enlarge
200%

Strawberry

Butterfly

Candy Corn

Painted Pumpkins

(page 19)
Size as needed

Houndstooth

Argyle

Gingerbread Haunted House

(page 46—47)

Enlarge
133%

Front

Wall

Base

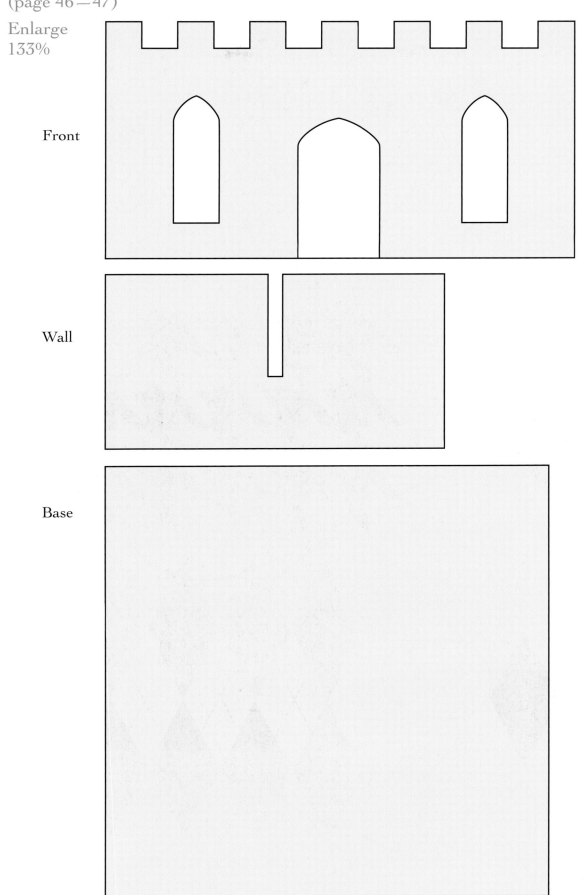

Animal Friends
(page 156)

Enlarge
133%

Pig Mask

Kitty Mask

Bird Mask

Terrorific Treat Bags

(page 157)

Enlarge 200%

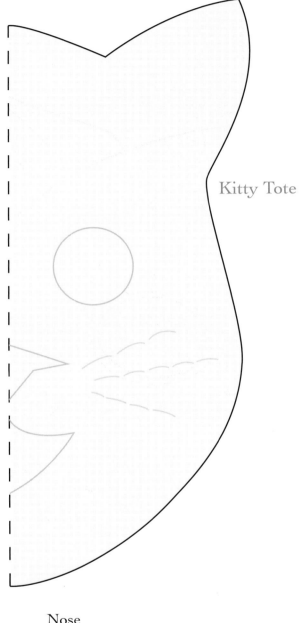

Kitty Tote

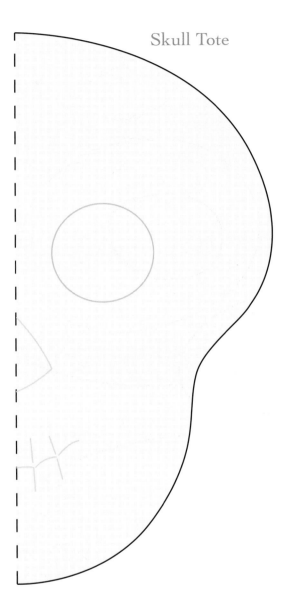

Skull Tote

Nose

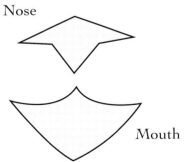

Mouth

Nose

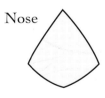

Little Miss Mermaid

(page 150)

Enlarge 200%

Bikini Shell
Insert
Cut 2
Blue

Bikini Shell
Cut 2
Pink

Bikini Shell
Cut 2
Light Blue

Insert
Cut 2
Light Blue

Waist

Skirt
Cut 2
Printed Fabric

Tail

Tail
Cut 2
Blue Felt

Night-Owl
(page 148–149)

Enlarge 200%

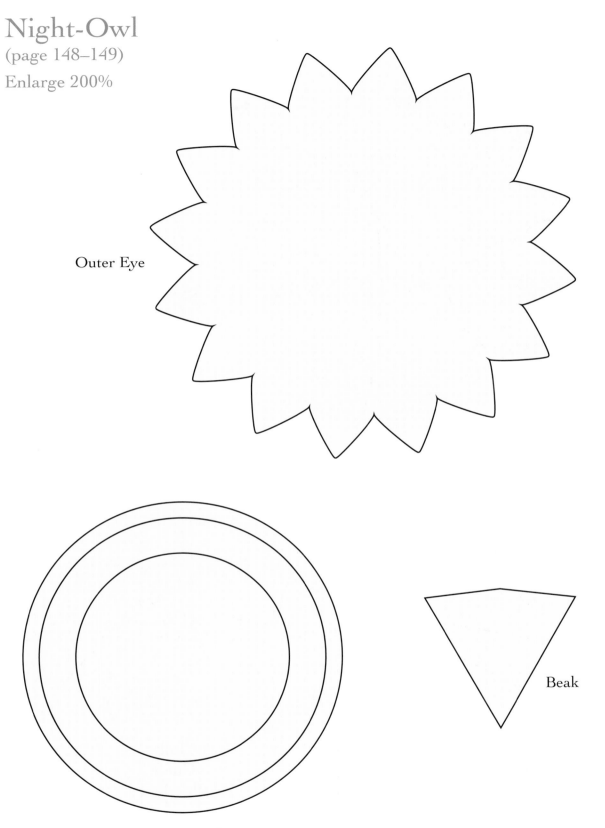

Outer Eye

Inner Eye Parts

Beak

continued on page 200

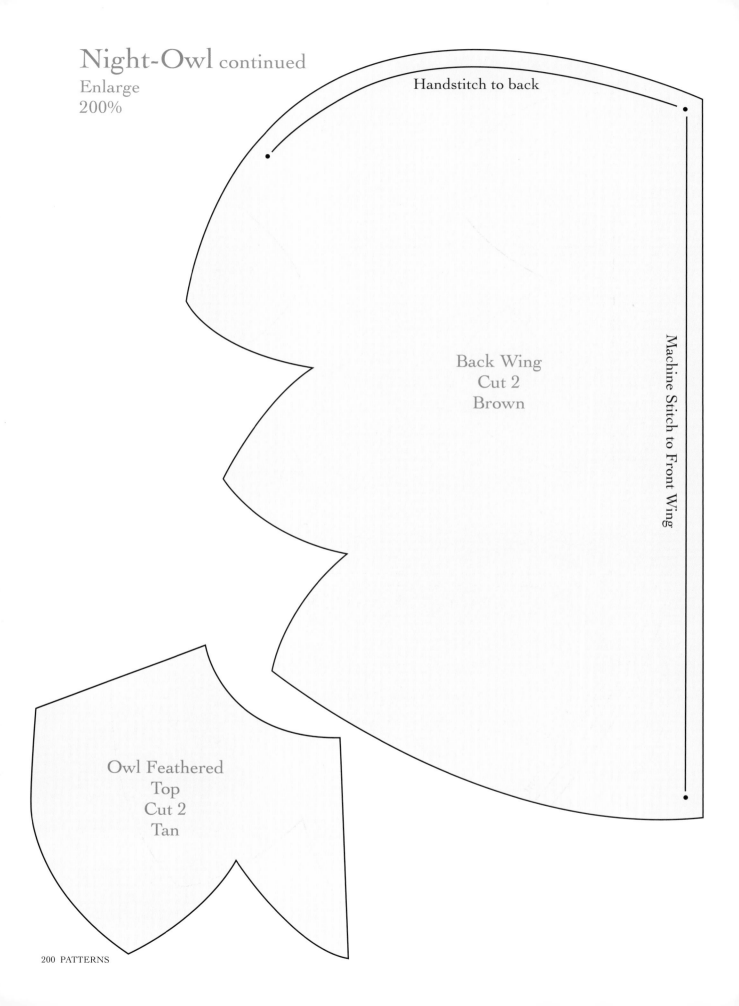

Night-Owl continued
Enlarge
200%

Handstitch to back

Back Wing
Cut 2
Brown

Machine Stitch to Front Wing

Owl Feathered
Top
Cut 2
Tan

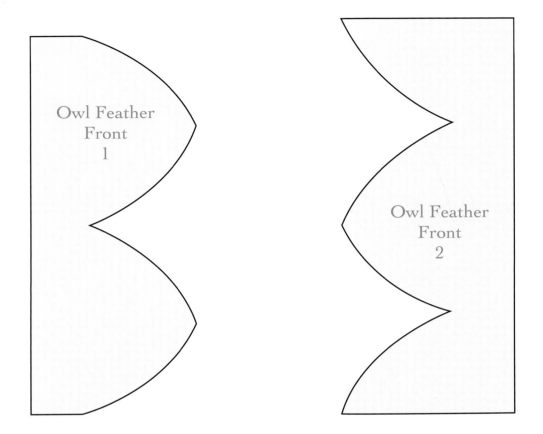

Owl Feather Front 1

Owl Feather Front 2

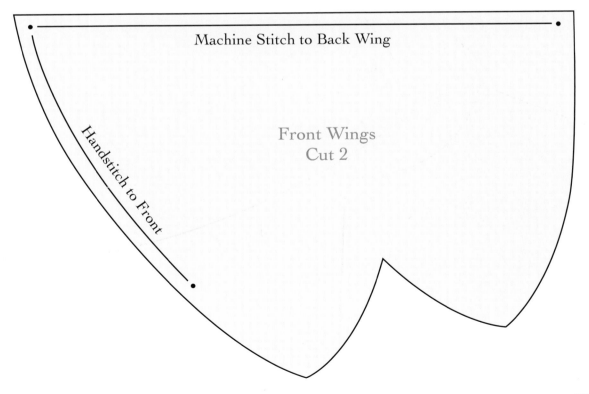

Machine Stitch to Back Wing

Handstitch to Front

Front Wings
Cut 2

A Little Squirrelly

(page 151)

Enlarge
200%

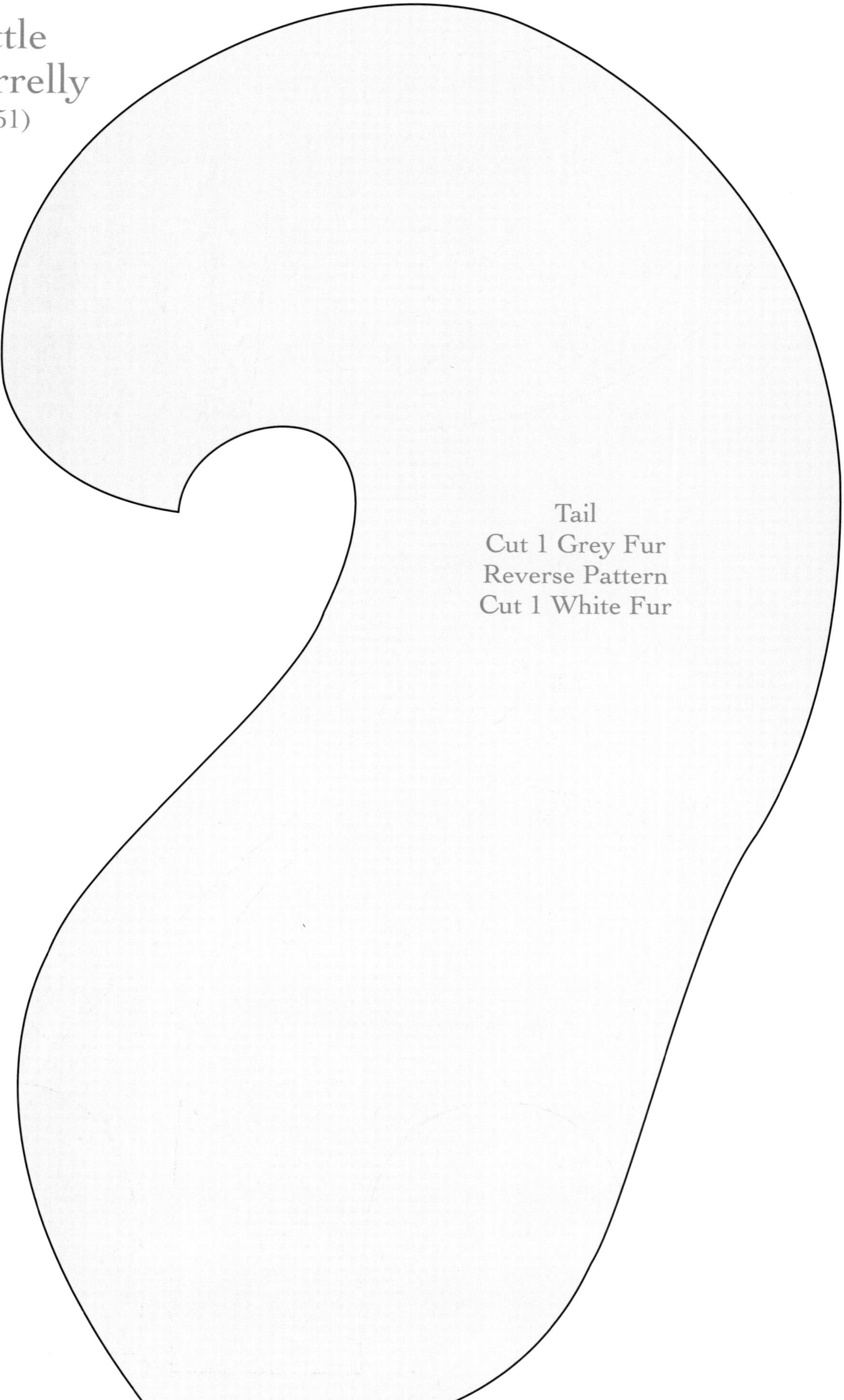

Tail
Cut 1 Grey Fur
Reverse Pattern
Cut 1 White Fur

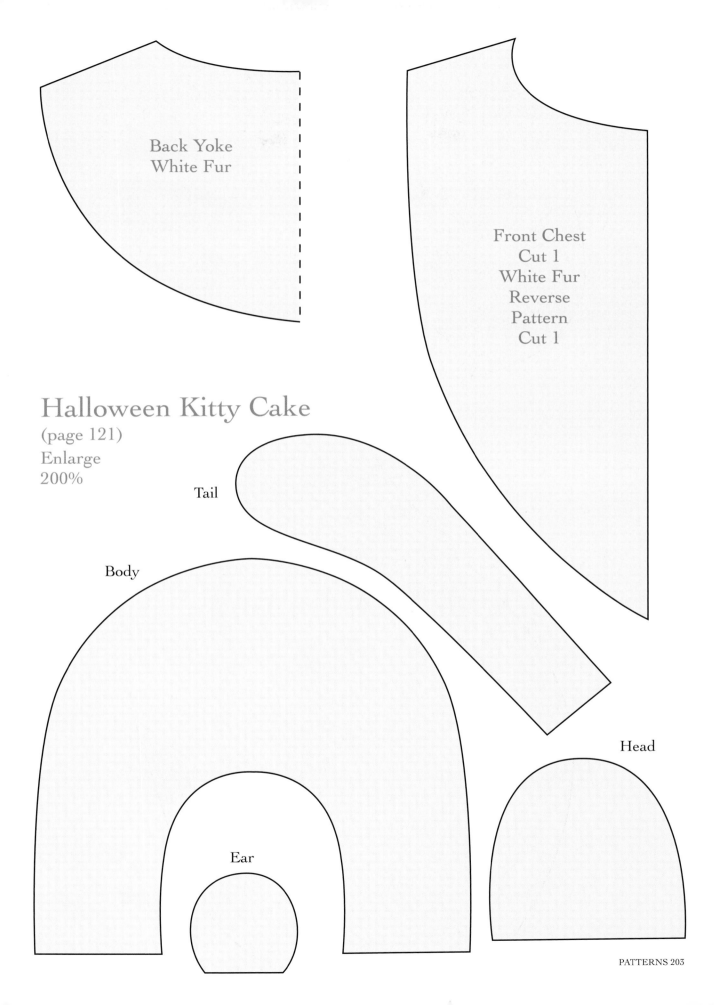

Back Yoke
White Fur

Front Chest
Cut 1
White Fur
Reverse
Pattern
Cut 1

Halloween Kitty Cake

(page 121)
Enlarge
200%

Tail

Body

Head

Ear

Halloween Cake Pokes

(pages 69, 75)

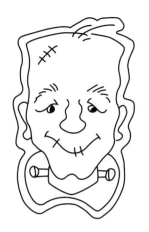

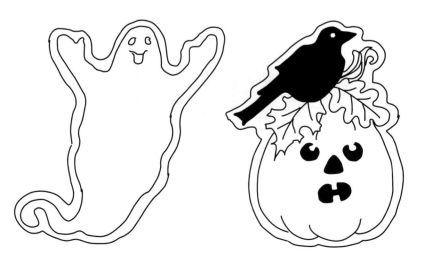

Resources:

www.bazzillbasics.com for papers, stickers and scrapbooking supplies

www.decadentfibers.com For wool roving and needlefelting supplies

www.earlmay.com For fish bowls

www.hersheystore.com For chocolate candies

www.hobbylobby.com For glass dishes, paints, markers, spray paints, jewels, pony beads, headbands, boas and general crafting supplies

www.jellybelly.com For candy corn and jelly beans

www.joann.com For fabrics, ribbons and other trims.

www.michaels.com For decoupage medium, adhesive letters, oval-shaped wooden piece, chenille stems and general crafting supplies

www.nationalnonwovens.com For felts and felting supplies

www.worldmarket.com For paper products and novelties

Credits:

THANKS TO ALL OF THOSE WHO HELPED CONCOCT THIS BOOK:

Photographers: Jay Wilde—Jay Wilde Photography, Dean Tanner—Primary Image; **Stylists:** Jennifer Peterson, Carol Field Dahlstrom, Jan Temeyer; **Food Professionals:** Jennifer Peterson, Holly Wiederin, Barbara Hoover, Carol Field Dahlstrom; **Models:** Sarah, Grace, Claire, Marcia, Elizabeth, Hadley Nan, Sophia, Izabel, Eva, Lillian, Elijah, Jordan, Roger; **Homes/Props:** Eunella Neymeyer, Donna Chesnut, Ardith Field, Roger Dahlstrom, Barbara Hoover; **Contributing Pattern Art:** Janet Pittman.

Project Index:

Recipe Index:

Appetizers & Snacks

Beverages